Wakefield Press

SILLINESS

Peter Timms was born in Melbourne and from 1971 until 1988 worked in public art museums in Victoria and NSW. He has been a freelance writer since 1988, including periods as editor of *Art Monthly Australia* and art critic for the *Age*. He has published eleven books, including one novel, *Asking for Trouble*. He now lives in Tasmania.

Also by Peter Timms

Australian Studio Pottery
The Nature of Gardens (editor)
Making Nature: Six Walks in the Bush
What's Wrong with Contemporary Art?
Philip Wolfhagen (artist's monograph)
Australia's Quarter Acre:
The Story of the Ordinary Suburban Garden
Private Lives: Australians at Home Since Federation
Hobart
House (with Robyn Stacey)
The Green Desert (with Peter Elfes)
Asking for Trouble (novel)

SILLINESS
A Serious History

Peter Timms

Wakefield Press

Wakefield Press
16 Rose Street
Mile End
South Australia 5031
www.wakefieldpress.com.au

First published 2019

Copyright © Peter Timms, 2019

All rights reserved. This book is copyright. Apart from
any fair dealing for the purposes of private study, research,
criticism or review, as permitted under the Copyright Act,
no part may be reproduced without written permission.
Enquiries should be addressed to the publisher.

Cover designed by Liz Nicholson, designBITE
Edited by Julia Beaven, Wakefield Press
Typeset by Michael Deves, Wakefield Press

ISBN 978 1 74305 645 5

 A catalogue record for this book is available from the National Library of Australia

 Wakefield Press thanks Coriole Vineyards for continued support

'There is nothing beside the Goodnesse of God, that preserves health so much as honest mirth, especially mirth used at dinner and supper, and mirth toward bed ...'   Introduction to *The Jests of Scoggin*, 1626

'... if the moderns mean by madness only a disturbance or transposition of the brain, by force of certain vapours issuing up from the lower faculties, then has this madness been the parent of all those mighty revolutions that have happened in empire, in philosophy, and in religion.'   Jonathan Swift, *A Tale of A Tub*

'"Contrarywise," continued Tweedledee, "if it was so, it might be; and if it were so, it would be; but as it isn't, it ain't. That's logic."'
Lewis Carroll, *Alice Through the Looking Glass*

'In the foolish and stupid, when carried to the highest degree, there is a sort of loftiness – *le sublime de la bêtise* ... "pure joy".'
V.G. Kuechelbecker

'"Why is 'lenguage' 'Ignatz'?"
"'Language' is, that we may understand each other."
"I would say, lenguage is, that we may mis-unda-stend each other."'   George Herriman, *Krazy Kat*

'There's nothing before our birth but an abyss, and there's only an abyss after our death. Our life is but a grain of sand in the indifferent ocean of infinity. So let's try to keep the moment from boredom and despair!'   Sergei Dovlatov, *The Suitcase*

Contents

Zero	WHAT TO EXPECT	ix
One	WHAT SILLINESS ISN'T	1
Two	HOW SILLINESS CHANGED THE WORLD	22
Three	TOO SILLY FOR WORDS	53
Four	ONLY DISCONNECT	87
Five	WORLDS WITHIN WORLDS	112
Six	ON AND ON AND ON	138
Seven	GETTING OUT OF HAND	164
Eight	THIS SILLY LIFE	197
	NOTES	225
	INDEX	228

Zero WHAT TO EXPECT

It was a fortuitous coming together of curiosity and cataracts that gave this book its appropriately offbeat beginning. While browsing in my local bookshop one afternoon, I happened upon a slim volume entitled *In Praise of Silliness*, and a light flashed on in my brain. Such a brilliant idea. Why on earth hadn't I thought of it? Only after I picked it up did I realise that poor eyesight had led me astray: it was Pico Iyer's *In Praise of Stillness*. So I have Mr Iyer to thank for unwittingly giving me my subject.

And what a rich and rewarding subject it has proven to be. As I delved, I discovered silliness everywhere. In the end, a huge amount had to be left out, and you will no doubt come up with your own list of things that should have been mentioned. Yet, while this book can only skim the surface, it will, I hope, give you an inkling of the great wealth of nonsense, absurdity, gobbledegook, blarney, bosh, tosh and amiable bunkum on offer to dispel melancholy and spark up our journey through life.

I should point out (in the unlikely event that it does not quickly become apparent) that I have no academic qualifications in literature, film, poetry, music, social history or any of the other disciplines that inform this book. Discipline has never been my forte. Although thoroughly researched (this is, after all, a 'serious history') it is not, by any stretch of the imagination, a scholarly tome. I hope I have managed to convey my boundless enthusiasm and my natural attraction to mischief and disruption in an entertaining and engaging way.

The main purpose of the book is to show that the kind of anarchic mayhem Monty Python and the Farrelly Brothers excel at is not uniquely modern but rather a recent chapter in a long and richly varied cultural narrative. However radical and inventive modern silliness might seem, you can be sure that someone in the eighteenth century, the sixteenth century or, indeed, the fourth century BC had thought of it before – or even outdone it. Historians usually pass over our ancestors' sophisticated delight in the ridiculous as if it were an embarrassment. So it is quite sobering to discover that today's brilliant originality is not as brilliantly original as we might have thought.

For practical reasons, I have limited myself to what is loosely called the Western World: Europe, Britain, America and Australia. This is not to say that Asia, Africa and everywhere else are devoid of silliness, only that to cover the globe would have exhausted my mental resources and your patience. There is probably more than enough here as it is. So, to the charge that this book is Eurocentric, I happily plead guilty. If the English are seen to dominate, that is because, when it comes to silliness, they just do. And if men are seen to dominate, well, again, that's because they just do, at least until the twentieth century, when film and television allowed women's silliness to finally get a look-in.

Please don't be put off by the absence of illustrations. Most of the films, books, poems and television programs I mention are available in one form or another on the internet. So keep your laptop on hand as a constant companion to your reading.

Finally, a note about structure: frankly, there isn't much. Chapter one is necessary background: a summary of what I think silliness is, and isn't, along with a brief outline of the standard approaches to humour. Chapter two is a power-romp through more than 2000 years of silliness, introducing some of the major figures I will be returning to later. All subsequent chapters are arranged thematically rather than chronologically and many of the key masters of silliness – Sterne, Carroll, Lear, Beckett, Joyce, O'Brien and especially Rabelais, the king of them all – crop up repeatedly in different guises.

The essays are meandering rather than systematic, obeying a loose, associative logic and occasionally wandering off into diversions and irrelevancies. This strikes me as appropriate for a book about silliness. Aristophanes and Cervantes rub shoulders with Spike Milligan and Peter Cook, Lewis Carroll and Jonathan Swift with Lucille Ball and Looney Tunes. While I believe the traditional distinction between high and low culture is useful and important in some contexts, it can only be a hindrance here.

All this jumping back and forth in time is bound to be a little discombobulating at first, and any attempt to read the whole book straight through may result in indigestion. I trust that the many funny examples quoted, along with your frequent detours into YouTube, will prove an effective antacid, encouraging you to persevere.

And when you do, you will, I'm sure, come to the paradoxical conclusion that although silliness is by definition frivolous and pointless it has had a profound impact on the tide of human affairs over millennia. For, as Simon Critchley points out in his book *On Humour*, it not only frees us from 'common sense', but exposes the misrepresentations, shortcuts and occlusions that common sense rests upon.

Peter Timms

One WHAT SILLINESS ISN'T

The world is awash with dumbness, lunacy, foolishness, insanity, inanity, mindlessness and idiocy. Plodding stupidity, which can pop up anywhere at any time, is something we are all distressingly capable of.

Silliness, on the other hand, is a refined and rare art with a quality all its own. Silliness is something to be savoured. But how to distinguish it from the common-or-garden madness that threatens to engulf us all? How do we recognise the occasional sparkling gem of pure silliness when it appears amongst the dross? This little book is here to help.

But it won't be straightforward. Silliness is a slippery concept: messy, unsettling and difficult to pin down. Its childish anarchy, its wilful disregard of social proprieties and constant frustration of our need for order put it outside our accustomed ways of perceiving the world, and thus dangerously into the orbit of anxiety, nihilism and the grotesque.

Yet, for all that, it can be great fun.

Embracing anarchy

We are not talking about jokes, most of which make sense (more or less) and conform to well established patterns. Even when we don't know what a joke's punchline will be, we can usually see it coming and how it is being arrived at. After all, a joke can thwart our expectations only after those expectations have been adequately established, and there are time-honoured ways of doing that.

Typically, a joke will begin with the set-up, for example: *ASIO is interviewing potential assassins and wants to test their obedience.* Then comes the exposition. This is often in three parts, with a stepped progression from one to the next, three being the minimum number required to establish a pattern. *To the first candidate they say, 'Here is a gun. Your wife is in the next room and we want you to go in there and shoot her.' The man refuses and fails the interview. The second man takes the gun, goes into the room, but soon emerges in tears. 'No, I'm sorry,' he says, 'I just can't do it.' The third candidate is a woman, whose husband is in the next room. After she goes in, there is a lot of shouting and banging. Finally, she emerges, exhausted.* And so to the punchline: *'Why didn't you tell me the gun wasn't loaded?' she gasps. 'I had to beat him to death with a chair leg.'* Most jokes make a point of some kind – here, about the supposed differences between the psychology of men and women. There is usually a moral in there somewhere, however dubious.

This is all very amusing, of course, but to the connoisseur of silliness, a little too neat and tidy: a little too predictable. What if one thing did not follow logically from another? What if nothing added up? That is, after all, what real life is like most of the time, however much we might wish it otherwise. Things don't always turn out the way we expect: there are no beginnings, middles or ends, and no punchlines (death excepted). Just when we think we've got all the chaos, muddle and confusion of daily life into some semblance of order, convinced that everything is under control, out of the blue we get hit by a bus, or struck by lightning, or fall pregnant, win the lottery, get mugged, get arrested, discover we are adopted, or meet the man or woman of our dreams. Turmoil and messiness take over and all our illusions of a manageable existence go out the window.

There are two ways of coping. One is to sink into despair and get morbidly drunk. The Russians have traditionally favoured this option. The other is to rejoice in our newfound freedom, embracing the myriad possibilities that life is capable of throwing at us and happily making the best of them; more the Italian way of going about things.

Think of silliness, then, as practice for dealing with the unexpected and unexplained. And the first step is to unhitch the safety belt of predictability and embrace anarchy and volatility. Jerry Lewis, interviewed in later life, said, 'Comedy in 1920 with the Keystone Cops had one ingredient that no one today takes into consideration – and this is silliness ... The woman is walking down the street, OK? She's got a huge package of groceries, and she's a very obese lady. The cop is standing there, and as she walks by him he makes a turn so he kicks her right in the ass. Well, that's so fuckin' mischievous! Her bag broke, the groceries went. See, today you'd have writers at Disney saying, "Why would the cop kick her in the ass?" Who *gives* a shit? Did you hear the laugh it got?'[1]

Actually, there was plenty of silliness around at the time. I suspect Lewis had been looking in the wrong places. But he very nicely nails the distinction between silliness and mere comedy.

Genre-busting

We like to know where we stand. We want to feel comfortable about which genre we're in. Is this a novel? If so, I expect characters, development and a satisfactory ending. If not (if reading Beckett or Houellebecq) then I have to be given fair warning. Is it a poem? Then I need to know if it's a sonnet or free verse, and whether or not it's meant to rhyme. A pop song should conform to the standard alternating chorus and verse format, and rhyme, and have a steady backbeat I can bob up and down to, and be about falling in or out of love. And when I download a movie, I search under comedy or drama or slasher, according to my mood.

If you really want to cause trouble, you can upturn these comfortable certainties by messing with genres. Remember the fracas when Bob Dylan went electric? And, if it's a laugh you want instead of a catcall, you do it *knowingly* and *mischievously*, signalling your comic intent so as to disarm any potential critics. For example, you could make a musical comedy about Adolf Hitler (like Mel Brooks), give a performance of Beethoven's *Moonlight Sonata* at Carnegie Hall that keeps veering uncontrollably into Col Porter's *Night and Day* (as Victor Borge did), or translate into French an English book on the history of Switzerland, adding cantankerous footnotes that gradually expand to completely overwhelm the original text (as Louis Raymond did in the eighteenth century). Or, at a simpler level, you might devise a limerick that suddenly stops being a limerick and turns into something else, while at the same time helpfully explaining why:

There was a young poet named Dan,
Whose lines would never quite scan.
When asked why it was,
He said, 'It's because
I always try to fit as many words into the last line as I
                                                possibly can.'

It's a form of trickery. Although comic intent has been signalled by the limerick form, we have, all the same, been led to expect one thing and been given something different. And we'll react either with anger (as Bob Dylan's folksy fans did) or with amusement, depending on how accommodating we feel and how we interpret the trickster's motives.

Silliness or nonsense?

Perhaps you'd rather call this kind of humour 'nonsense'. Most people do. Edward Lear, usually credited with being the inventor of literary silliness, called his most famous collection *A Book of Nonsense*. All the same, there is, I think, a subtle distinction. When we call something nonsense, we mean it doesn't follow logic, and logic – from *logos*, 'the word' – is a method of reasoning and arguing from certain principles or conventions. So, it would be odd to call John Cleese's famous silly walk a nonsense walk, or to describe a piece of music as nonsense (except, perhaps, as a way of dismissing it as no good). Music is not about 'making sense' in the strict meaning of the term. On the other hand, there are many examples of musical *silliness*: Mozart's *A Musical Joke* is silly, as well as some of Haydn's quartets, and the Goons' *Ying Tong Song*.

While silliness can include slapstick, dance, mime or even

just facial expressions, nonsense more specifically refers to a violation – intentional or otherwise – of logical thought. Admittedly, the distinction is a fine one, and in practice the two words are often used interchangeably. Except in chapter three, which is about nonsense words, I intend to stick with 'silliness'. I like its jauntiness, its lightness and levity, and the fact that it is less judgemental, without the negative connotations of 'non-sense'.

The word 'silly' has had a chequered career. From about 1350 to the mid 1600s, it could have one of three related, yet quite distinct, meanings: deserving of pity and sympathy; weak and insignificant (especially as applied to women, children or newborn lambs); or simple, rustic and ignorant. As the Oxford Dictionary complains, it can sometimes be difficult to work out what meaning a writer intended. Over time, the definition narrowed into 'foolish', 'empty-headed' and 'imbecilic', usually meant disparagingly. Nevertheless, using silliness to deliberately evoke laughter is noted as early as the 1590s.

During the nineteenth century, 'silly' often meant 'stunned' or 'stupefied' as the result of a blow to the head. Hence 'silly mid-on' in cricket, where the fielder is so close to the batsman as to be almost guaranteed a concussion. Our present interpretation, 'to act foolishly' – or, as Kipling nicely puts it, 'to silly about' – also comes into common use at this time. The Oxford Dictionary doesn't say, but I suspect that it is at least partly under the influence of children's literature over the past 150 years or so that the word has gained its aura of fondness and sympathetic indulgence.

All of which brings us, by a circuitous route, to our first principle of silliness: it thumbs its nose at the conventions of form, refusing to obey the rules – refusing, in fact, to acknowledge that there are any rules. Silliness is freewheeling and unstructured, deliberately sabotaging our expectations.

Silliness is pointless

Milan Kundera (with tongue in Czech, perhaps), said that satire is the lowest form of wit because it has a point. The English writer Jonathan Coe claims that it is also destined to fail. 'The Winshaw Prize', a segment of his novel *Number 11*, revolves around a plot to kill a satirist because satirists always make things worse. 'Political humour is the very opposite of political action,' the killer blogs. 'Not just its opposite but its mortal enemy.'[2] *Number 11* is, as you might have guessed, a satire. Peter Cook made the same point with characteristic aplomb in 1961, when he opened The Establishment, his London comedy club. He said he was inspired by the Berlin cabarets of the 1930s that had done so much to stop the rise of Adolf Hitler and prevent the Second World War.

Yet today, satire flourishes as never before. Despite all the evidence, there are still those who believe society can be laughed into reform. Here's the rub: good satirists, however savage, must be half in love with their targets, or at the very least hold them in grudging respect. You don't satirise politics to pour scorn on the entire political system, but rather in the hope of cleaning it up and making it better. That demands faith in the system and its capacity for reform. You must have enough regard for politics, and enough insider knowledge, to feel motivated. Not only that, but your audience must share at least some of your interest and knowledge. Thus, when Armando Iannucci, creator and writer of the BBC political comedy *The Thick of It*, was asked whether he thought the series had changed anything, he replied, 'I think it has. It's brought the way politics functions in this country out into the open. It shows the government needs a bit more transparency, but it also helps you feel for the politicians sometimes. They are just ordinary people trying to do a job.' (If the characters in *The Thick of It* are just ordinary people, then heaven help us all!) This is what satire is meant to do. Yet, can anyone point to a single improvement in the practice of politics or in public attitudes to politicians since *The Thick of It* was screened?

I can't imagine that Screaming Lord Sutch, the founder of Britain's Official Monster Raving Loony Party, would have wanted to make any such claim. The only point he was trying to make (if it can be called a point) is that politics is incapable of redemption and there's not a damn thing anyone can do about it. That isn't meant to be helpful. According to Sutch, and the ACT's Sun Ripened Warm Tomato Party, Canada's Fed-Up Party, Denmark's Union of Conscientiously Work-Shy Elements, and the Hungarian Two-Tailed Dog Party (which promises eternal life, world peace, one work day a week, two sunsets a day in various colours, and free beer), withering scorn is really the only possible response to modern-day politics.

While satire takes a stand, setting out to right wrongs, silliness is cheerfully non-judgemental, on the understanding that everything is absurd and futile and the sooner we all come to terms with this and surrender ourselves to it the better off we will be. If satire speaks truth to power, as the cliché has it, then silliness speaks a language power will never understand. (I'll come back to this point in a minute.)

Of course, silliness is often a component of satire and it's not always clear where one ends and the other begins. Many of the writers who will feature in this book are satirists – Aristophanes, Rabelais, Cervantes, Sterne, Gogol and so on – but they are not just satirists. They also take off into glorious flights of silliness whenever the mood takes them, so it would seem churlish, and misleading, to neglect them on that score. At heart, however, satire and silliness have quite distinct aims. The fundamental distinction is that satire carries with it the whiff of reformist zeal, whereas silliness doesn't give a damn.

So, the second principle of silliness is that it must be, or at least appear to be, pointless. There is no message, no moral, no hidden agenda. As we shall see, the reality is a good deal more complicated (strictly speaking, nothing is ever entirely pointless) but that, anyway, is the conceit and it will do for the time being.

Silly or stupid?

When a university cancels a Mexican-themed staff party, complete with sombreros, following a complaint from a student body called the Autonomous Collective Against Racism, or a reactionary politician insists on a link between abortion and breast cancer, or when Air Force officials in Georgia (USA) advertise a weekend 'Fun Shoot' in honour of committed pacifist Martin Luther King Jnr (there is no shortage of examples to choose from), these people are being stupid. Yet they would not take kindly to that being pointed out. In their endearingly naïve way, they think they are behaving rationally. Their stupidity is unintentional, it just comes naturally to them.

You might take exception to my examples. Stupidity is a relative concept and one person's stupidity is another's common sense. Yet, whatever targets we choose to apply it to, we are bound to think of it as an absence of mental capacity with potentially damaging consequences. Stupidity is not, by anyone's definition, a positive attribute.

As I mentioned, we are all capable of acting stupidly from time to time, but when we do, we can usually admit our lapse, apologise profusely and try to put it behind us, or cover it up and pretend it never happened. That is not the same as calling someone a stupid person, which implies that it is ingrained. To call someone stupid is much more damning than pointing out that they have acted stupidly.

When it comes to silliness, the distinction is much less clear-cut. 'You are being silly' and 'you are silly' mean pretty much the same thing, and you'd have to be very thin-skinned to interpret either as insulting. Not only is calling someone silly less hurtful than calling them stupid, it is in most cases a term of endearment, particularly when applied to children. Silliness is playful and harmless.

Silliness, at least the kind this book is interested in, is not the unfortunate by-product of a lack of grey matter. Quite the opposite: it frequently comes from highly developed intellects. Four of the six members of Monty Python, for example, were Oxford or Cambridge graduates (if that is a measure of highly developed intellect). Silliness is a transgressive response to normality.

Which brings us to the third principle of silliness: it must be intentional. This is not to say that we can't sometimes find things silly that were never intended to be, but, for the purposes of this book, the irrationality must be deliberate and knowing, usually (although, as we will see, not always) just for the sake of a laugh. It is not a failure but rather a vexatious subversion of common sense. It is anything but stupid.

In fact, I'd go further and say that it can be a very effective weapon against stupidity. By choosing to embrace incoherence and inappropriateness, and by airing our opposition to the norms, we are effectively claiming intellectual and moral superiority. This, it has to be admitted, is not always an edifying spectacle. It's hard to avoid the accusation that there is often an element of social posturing in acting silly. It can be self-congratulatory to laugh at something others just don't get.

Like all power, this can become addictive and, like all addictions, it makes ever-increasing demands. Transgression quickly becomes the norm (think of how quickly Monty Python's most inane utterances were being drunkenly bandied about in pubs), meaning that ever more extreme forms are needed to provide the high. Silliness constantly has to negotiate its relationships to cultural norms, which is why it is so difficult to pin down.

Why we laugh

Why do we find some things amusing and not others? What provokes the laughter response?

Such questions are as old as laughter itself. And the results of centuries of debate by some of history's most profound (although, it must be said, least amusing) thinkers are generally herded together under three, or possibly four, thematic umbrellas. None is entirely satisfying, but they are the best explanations we've got.

The first, Superiority Theory, maintains that laughter is all about power. It was formulated by Aristotle, boosted by

Thomas Hobbes in the seventeenth century, and has since been given a shot in the arm by Foucault, who thought everything was about power – or, as he would put it, Power. This may well be, I suppose, if you choose to see the world that way. The British are contemptuous of colonials, Australians belittle New Zealanders, middle-aged men tease their mothers-in-law, Charles Atlas types kick sand in five-stone weaklings' faces (at least they used to), kids ridicule oldies on mobility scooters, and everyone laughs at dogs humping in the park. There are strictly policed grades of acceptability, depending upon how sensitive the target of the joke is perceived to be: Irish jokes are still pretty much okay, on the understanding that the Irish are quite capable of looking after themselves; gay jokes are now on the cusp of unacceptability, a pity given that the Gay Liberation movement was originally the essence of self-mockery; and almost anything to do with race is a no-go zone. It is our great misfortune to be living in a humourless age in which being offended has become a competitive sport and even the most innocuous jibe risks not a laugh but a lawsuit.

Superiority Theory is more acceptable in reverse – the weak making fun of the strong – on the quite reasonable assumption that the rich and powerful deserve all they get. Bringing politicians down a peg or two is always good for a laugh, but there's fun in seeing any figures of social standing suffer a blow to their dignity. When a BBC radio commentator innocently observed after a boat race that the wife of the Cambridge captain was kissing the cox of the Oxford crew, it was the image of the respectable lady on her knees in public that made it so comical.

The Queen is the ideal subject, of course, surrounded as she is by elaborate pomp and ceremony signifying nothing. As Mr Bean lines up to greet her at a film premiere, he quivers with anxiety, fretting about his shoes being shiny enough, his breath fresh enough and his fingernails properly trimmed. The tension rises as the royal personage, swathed in blue and with a tiara perched on her head, makes her way down the line towards him, and he just manages to extract his finger from his fly as she steps before him to extend a welcoming hand. Panicking, he lurches forward in a deep, well-practised bow, and head-butts her so violently she flies backwards into the crowd of onlookers.

The second theory of humour, championed by Kant, Schopenhauer and Kierkegaard, who all expounded it with immense solemnity, is Incongruity Theory. This maintains that we are amused when our expectations are thwarted (as in genre-busting, mentioned earlier). We expect one outcome but get another and it is our surprise, and perhaps embarrassment, that makes us laugh. It applies especially well to jokes, where the punchline subverts the set-up. For example: *A man in a movie theatre is intrigued by a fox terrier belonging to an old lady sitting in front of him, which hardly takes its eyes off the screen. When the lights go up, he leans forward and says, 'Excuse me, but I couldn't help noticing your dog. He actually seemed to be enjoying the film.' 'Yes,' she replies, 'I was amazed too. He hated the book.'*

Incongruity Theory is straightforward enough, and is the most widely accepted of the three today. However, as with Superiority Theory (which doesn't cover puns and other forms of wordplay, for example) there is humour it cannot adequately account for, such as mime and clowning. It also fails to explain the many instances of thwarted expectations that are anything but funny. Bob Dylan's fans were certainly not amused on

Silliness: A Serious History

25 July 1965. So why do we laugh at some and not others?

Thirdly, there is Release Theory, which goes back to the eighteenth century but whose most famous proponent was Freud. Laughter releases pent-up energy, like a pressure valve in a steam boiler. This, said Freud, is why so many jokes are about sex or hostility. When we laugh at them, however, it is not repressed sexuality or hostility as such that we are releasing, but the emotions that normally repress them. It's a fine distinction, and the details needn't detain us here. Basically, what Freud is saying is that our amusement at the ineptness of a clown, for example, lets go the energy we use in worrying about how we should be conducting ourselves in public, and when we tell a racist joke or laugh guiltily at something that crosses the boundaries of good taste, we release some of the hostility we usually keep bottled up.

It doesn't even have to be funny to be funny. Some fifty or so years ago, the American comedian Lenny Bruce would point accusingly at members of his audience and shout 'nigger' or 'spic' or 'kike', until everyone was helpless with laughter. It was, said the writer, Leonard Michaels, 'as if we'd all gone over the edge, crazed by the annihilation of proprieties, or whatever had kept us from this until now'. So maybe Freud was on to something.

Indeed, it is liberating to witness someone other than us airily undermining political correctness: doing what we would love to do if only we had the courage. In an episode of Ricky Gervais's television series *Extras*, Ben Stiller is directing a film based on the life of a man whose mother was brutally murdered during the Balkans War. On set as an adviser, the distraught man breaks down in tears after every take, garnering the heartfelt sympathy of actors and crew. Stiller's frustration with these emotional outbursts builds until, unable to take any more, he looks the sobbing man squarely in the eye and shouts, 'For God's sake, will you shut up about your fucking mother!' We've all been there. Fortunately we are usually constrained by a fear of causing offence or getting punched on the nose. Only if you're a stickler for the social proprieties will you fail to be amused.

And that, as it happens, is where Release Theory starts to break down. If we laugh to release emotions that normally repress sexual or racist feelings, then a clergyman would be expected to laugh more heartily at a racist or sexual joke than a wharf labourer, which, even allowing for my shameless typecasting, is plainly not the case.

Thomas Aquinas brings us to a fourth possible theory of humour, which equates it with play ('possible' because it seems not to have been fully embraced by scholars, although it strikes me as the most appealing). In moderation – however that might be defined – play and humour are simply restful and restorative and make you a happy person who is pleasant to be with. 'It is against reason', Aquinas writes, 'for a man to be burdensome to others, by never showing himself agreeable to others or being a killjoy or wet blanket on their enjoyment'. So, laughter and humour simply give us pleasure. It's easy to see why philosophers, whose job it is to find an underlying purpose for everything, are not so keen on this theory. Humour is just for pleasure? Surely not, there must be more to it than that!

Well, yes, there is. You have only to observe children and young animals, for whom play is important in learning how to compete and cooperate, how to accept the rules, and how to bracket-off certain activities from day-to-day life. And the exaggerated guffaws at a backyard barbecue signal that laughter is an essential part of adult human bonding. It's about belonging. We're much more likely to laugh at a funny movie as a member of an audience than watching it at home alone, and although a book might be promoted as 'laugh-out-loud', it probably won't be unless we are reading it out loud in a group, preferably after a couple of glasses of wine. So, play and humour are educative tools for the young and socialising tools for their elders.

Much depends on context. Recognising the distinction between play and normal life (something that today, as a society, we seem increasingly unwilling to do) is crucial. For instance, in winter, the good citizens of Hobart like to drive to the top of Mount Wellington and throw snowballs at each other. It is wonderfully silly. Hurling projectiles at complete strangers anywhere else, even soft things that don't hurt, would invite arrest, but in the snow the rules are different and everyone takes such harmless physical assault in good grace, although I await the first lawsuit from some offended killjoy who fails to understand the distinction.

Where silliness fits

So, where does silliness fit among these four theories?

It's not easy to say for certain. Take a straightforward example, a riddle I learned at primary school, which, although not particularly funny, is perfectly silly:

> *What's the difference between a duck?*
> *One of its legs is both the same.*

What Silliness Isn't

I suppose this fits with Incongruity Theory, but only in the sense that, like the limerick I quoted earlier, it plays merry havoc with our expectations of what a riddle is supposed to be, and I doubt Schopenhauer or Kierkegaard would have taken it under their wings. It sets up no expectations of its own; both question and answer are linguistically incoherent and bear little relationship to one another; there is no satisfactory set-up and no punchline. The best we can say is that it is a bit of harmless wordplay of the kind to tickle the fancy of a six-year-old.

A cartoon by Paul Crum (who is often cited as an important influence on Spike Milligan and John Cleese), first published in *Punch* in the late 1930s, is arguably both silly and funny. It shows two hippopotamuses submerged in a placid pool with just their snouts and eyes breaking the surface. One is remarking casually to the other, 'I keep thinking it's Tuesday.' This cartoon is now famous. It even has its own Wikipedia entry. But does it fit any of our categories? Well, again, Incongruity Theory applies to some extent because, assuming we accept that a hippopotamus could speak, that is not what we would expect it to say. All the same, it's not quite right, is it. It's as if Crum didn't understand how a joke was meant to work. All his cartoons leave this curious impression that we might have missed something, or that he has. In another, a distinguished-looking fellow at a gentlemen's club leans over to the man next to him and says, 'Would it interest you to see my son's report?' 'No', is the stern reply. Why is this funny? I have no idea, and nor, I'm sure, would Freud, Schopenhauer or Kant.

I don't know if the American humorist James Thurber was familiar with Crum's cartoons, but the two men share a very particular sense of what's funny. Like Crum, Thurber is keen on animals behaving like pragmatic, not-very-bright people: the polar-bear cub, for instance, who complains to its parents, 'I don't care what you say, I'm cold!' Or the mole confronting another in a tunnel, who says, 'I backed up the last time.' My favourite Thurber cartoon shows a stern-looking woman confronting an enormous hippo, which has a pipe, a hat and a discarded shoe at its feet and a self-satisfied smirk on its face. 'What have you done with Dr Millmoss?' she demands. Judged according to any of the standard theories, these cartoons simply don't work. Yet, they do. And Thurber's spiky, barely competent drawings add to their delightful sense of brittleness.

What scholars tend to do is to look at existing forms of humour and base their theories on what they find. Primarily they look at jokes, as the title of Freud's book, *Jokes and Their Relation to the Unconscious*, confirms. They mean jokes of the standard set-up-exposition-punchline format. Anything that violates the accepted patterns – anything anarchic, oddball and silly – is bound to slip under their radar.

So, why bother?

To recap: silliness is genre-busting, deliberately flouting expectations; it is intentionally pointless and superficial, seeking nothing more than a good laugh; it makes no sense; and it carelessly tramples on everyone's sensitivities. So, why bother with it at all?

Well, for one thing, the senseless represents a healthy assault on the proper and predictable. In this obsessively pragmatic and materialistic age, in which everything is expected to directly contribute to our physical and social wellbeing, it takes us back to the simple, undirected play of childhood. It frees us, if only for a short while, from the tyranny of rationalism.

This is something we need, today more than ever. To be taken seriously, novels, films, plays, works of art and even ballets must be 'about' (or must 'address') some social or political issue, usually in ways that bolster the fashionable liberal view. When a novel wins a prize, it will be because it has 'something important to tell us' rather than because it's a bloody good read, and the more depressing and distressing that message, the better its chances. Thank goodness, then, for the French *Prix de la Page 112*, which is what it says it is: an award for the best page 112 in a new book. The administrators of the prize claim that at about page 112, a book is liable to lose energy. 'The reader is apt to neglect page 112, that is why we chose it.' But such clear-headedness is rare. The arts are much more likely to take their cue from the news media. Even children's books have succumbed to hectoring polemics about gender re-alignment, bullying, environmental destruction or stranger-danger.

Surely we are capable of more generosity of spirit. We are more than just our bodies and our social interactions. Why should we be defined by our tragedies and shortcomings? Why must we be cowed into thinking that the alleviation of suffering and injustice, however important, is all we are capable of? Occasionally, we need to open a window and take a breath of air, to stretch our imaginations and discover our creative potential: in short, to be joyful, just for the hell of it.

Humour, especially silly humour, lifts us out of our accustomed moral frameworks and lets us see the world from a fresh perspective. It combats pessimism, saves us from self absorption and egotism, and reminds us there's more to life than what we do and what happens to us. In short, it makes us better people.

That's quite a lot. But there's more. Silliness is also an essential irritant. There are, after all, people who deserve to be irritated, particularly those annoying busybodies who love to control other people's lives: politicians, business executives, religious leaders and the like. They long ago proved themselves impervious to outrage, resentment or even rational argument. Violent revolt will only harden their resolve and satire flatters them with attention. Only silliness is capable of getting under their skin, even as they pretend to ignore it. Silliness is the banana skin on the footpath, the fart at the dinner party, the irrelevance in the room. Simply by failing to acknowledge their authority – or indeed their very existence – it undermines their self esteem, erodes their sense of control and leaves them stranded. On this basis, Spike Milligan's *Ying Tong Song* is more subversive than a Molotov cocktail.

On 11 November 1975, Prime Minister Gough Whitlam appeared on the steps of Parliament House in Canberra to announce to a baying crowd that he had just been sacked by the Governor-General. It was a big moment in Australian politics and, as luck would have it, one of the country's most irreverent comedians was there, shamelessly hogging the limelight. Although Norman Gunston (the alter ego of Gary McDonald) said nothing particularly funny, his clownish antics put him in stark contrast to the pompous self-importance of everyone around him. The reactions of the party heavies were revealing. Bob Hawke, then Federal President of the Labor Party, snapped, 'I think it's a bit too serious for that,' and abruptly turned his back. Whitlam ignored Gunston altogether, although they were standing side-by-side. Only future Labor leader, Bill Hayden, made an effort. 'I think you're sending me up,' he said, as cheerfully as possible, although he was clearly rattled. That was exactly what Gunston was doing, of course – sending him up – in a way that Hayden couldn't deal with. Powerful people thrive on opposition. They enjoy being criticised, even feared, and they don't mind being hated, but being ignored is simply too much for their fragile egos.

So, while silliness might be pointless in the sense that it does not have a stated purpose and doesn't promote any particular point of view, it is not without effect. Its ability to prick pomposity and undermine self-importance is, in itself, reason enough to treasure it.

The last word should go to M.A. Screech, the distinguished translator of Rabelais:

> To blubber instead of working hard is ignoble, and can be turned into a subject of laughter. To prefer your bum to your mind is odd, and can be turned into a subject of laughter. To worship human beings or objects is idolatrous and can be turned into a subject of laughter. To interpret words and other signs wrongly is misleading, and can be turned into a subject of laughter. As for cruelty, in a farce it almost always is the subject of laughter. Both birth and death are veiled with awe: stripped of their veils and skilfully trivialised, they too can be turned into subjects of laughter.[3]

Before we dive in to experience that laughter at firsthand, we need to take a quick caper through history, just to put things into perspective.

Two HOW SILLINESS CHANGED THE WORLD

Antique silliness

We are all capable of enjoying a good laugh, be it a titter, snigger, chuckle, guffaw or, all too rarely, an unseemly bout of full-throated, double-up-and-gasp-for-air hysterics of the kind that makes you think you're going to die laughing. Although obviously some people have more occasion for it than others, laughter is universal, and possibly unique to humans (chimpanzees might be capable of it, but hyenas and kookaburras are only pretending). This is not to say that animals can't have a sense of humour, only that they can't physically laugh.

The ancients, so often painted as a dour and self-important lot, loved social satire, parody, obscenity and farce. At least, we know the Greeks and Romans did: there are sure to have been Phoenician and Babylonian tricksters and mischief-makers as well. William Hansen, an American classicist, has collected hundreds of ancient Greek and Roman stories, anecdotes, jokes and jibes, including scabrous songs sung by soldiers just out of the emperor's earshot during triumphal processions, snippets and anecdotes from prominent authors such as Aristophanes and Apuleius, anonymous graffiti, and the kinds of stories men like to swap after a few drinks.[4] You come away convinced that the ancients knew how to enjoy themselves.

Aristophanes gave the Greeks plenty to laugh at. His plays are a riot of puns, *non-sequiturs*, insults and off-the-wall nonsense. Plutarch in the first century AD advised against quoting him at dinner parties. Aristophanes' plays, he fumed, were full of 'verbal diarrhoea and plain sickening rubbish', an assessment Aristophanes himself might have cheerfully agreed with.

As his translators David Barrett and Alan Sommerstein point out, much of his wordplay is unavailable to us today because it is untranslatable. However, they give us a taste with delightful passages like this little ditty sung by the chorus in *The Birds*:

> *The Skiapods, or Ombripeds*
> *Are most engaging fellers:*
> *They hold their feet above their heads*
> *And use them as umbrellas.*
>
> *They live beside a stagnant lake,*
> *Where Socrates – just fancy! –*
> *Instructs his half-starved pupils in*
> *The art of necromancy.*
>
> *Peisander saw him work the trick*
> *And said 'Oh please repeat it!*
> *I lost my spirit long ago;*
> *I'd dearly love to meet it.'*
>
> *'Then slay,' the unwashed sage replied,*
> *'A lamb – but no, a lamb'll*
> *Be much too small a sacrifice;*
> *You'd better slay a camel.'*[5]

SILLINESS: A SERIOUS HISTORY

In *The Frogs*, Aristophanes indulges in a bit of mischief at the expense of two of Greece's most respected tragedians. The joke hinges on extended play with the two meanings of 'weight'. Aeschylus and Euripides, both long dead, are arguing in the underworld about who is (or was) the better poet. Aeschylus finally proposes that the matter be settled once and for all by putting their poetry on the scales to see whose is the weightier. A set of scales being duly produced, each man leans over one of the two pans to recite a line of verse. Euripides begins with: 'If only Argo had never winged its way ...', Aeschylus with: 'The watery vale of Spercheius, where cattle graze ...' The scales tip firmly in Aeschylus' favour. Dionysus, who is moderating the debate, explains: 'He put in a river, like the wool merchants who wet their wool to make it weigh more, whereas you with your "winged its way" ...' So they try again. This time, Aeschylus's line makes reference to death, while Euripides tries: 'Persuasion has no temple other than the word ...' Death is, of course, 'the heaviest burden of all', so Aeschylus wins again. 'What about Persuasion?' Euripides objects. 'Doesn't that carry any weight? So beautifully phrased too.' 'No,' Dionysus replies gravely, 'Persuasion is hollow. It has no substance of its own. You'll have to think of something with real gravity to weigh your side down. Something huge and hulking.' Euripides, who sports a prosthetic phallus, typical of characters in old Greek comedy, muses to himself, 'What have I got that's huge and hulking? Hmm, let me think ...' And on it goes, with Euripides being outclassed every time.[6] Aristophanes seems to have had it in for Euripides, whom he pillories in several of his plays. Perhaps he just thought the high seriousness of tragedy was fair game.

Many comic authors over the next 2000 years or so,

including Rabelais, Laurence Sterne, Flann O'Brien and Edward Lear, were well schooled in the classics, so the echoes of Aristophanes we find in their work are hardly coincidental. 'And he went flying off, taking the doormat with him,' says a character in *The Frogs*. 'He never could resist a nice doormat,' his companion observes. This could easily be mistaken for one of Flann O'Brien's absurdist exchanges.

By the time Plautus was cracking up his fellow Romans towards the end of the third century BC, Aristophanes was a classic, or a dirty old fart, depending on where you stood. The Roman masses of the early Republic, like the Americans of the 1950s, stood firmly on the puritanical and conservative side. They had little taste for political satire or sexual shenanigans; they just wanted some good clean fun and Plautus was happy to oblige. His exuberant farces, full of wit, mockery, music and charm, take familiar themes of love, domestic strife, cheating and one-upmanship and reflect them to his audience through a fairground distorting mirror.

Not for him Aristophanes' fantasies about birds building cities in the sky (the origin of our expression 'cloud-cuckoo-land'). Plautus's feet remain firmly on the ground, so it is difficult to extract one-liners. It's his absurdly convoluted plots that provide the merriment. In *The Braggart Soldier*, much fun is had at the expense of a handsome young officer's overweening vanity, which, of course, is finally his undoing. 'If any of you knows a man more full of bull or empty boastings,' his slave pleads to the audience, 'you can have me – free of tax. But I'll say this: I'm crazy for his olive salad!' *The Brothers Menaechmus*, one of Plautus's best-known works, turns on the confusion between identical twin brothers, one an upright citizen, the other a wastrel who, somewhat implausibly, are unaware of each other's existence, leading to merry chaos. From a modern perspective, it does go on a bit, but with some judicious honing it could easily pass muster as a modern sitcom. Shakespeare adapted it for *A Comedy of Errors* and Rodgers and Hart for *The Boys from Syracuse*. The 1960s musical *A Funny Thing Happened on the Way to the Forum* is mostly from Plautus, too.

He counts as silly for us today because he is blithely unconcerned about making a point or drawing a moral: he just wants to entertain. His plays are farcical, irreverent and corny, always ending happily, with the implausibilities smoothed away and the warring characters reconciled. Plautus popularised the 'boy meets girl/loses girl/is reunited with girl' plot that Hollywood has been milking for decades. And he came up with many of the stock characters we recognise today: the morally upright couple whose relationship is undermined by their racier best friend; the scheming rival; the henpecked husband; the rebellious son; and the servant (or, for Plautus, slave) who is a lot more savvy than his master (think Jeeves and Bertie Wooster). Although Aristophanes also makes good use of that last character, in Plautus, himself a former slave, he reigns supreme. Any real slaves who behaved as Palaestrio and Sceledrus do in *The Braggart Soldier* would have been put to death, but in Plautus's topsy-turvy world they triumph.

Idiots were a favourite target of Roman humour. In a popular joke, a man complains, 'The slave you sold me died,' and the idiot replies, 'That's funny, he never did anything like that when I owned him.' Another tells of identical twin brothers. After one of them dies, the idiot sees the survivor in the street and asks, 'Was it you who died, or your brother?' Professor Hansen gives us several more of similar ilk. While not, strictly speaking, silly from my point of view, these jokes do have a certain daffy charm.

Roman practical jokes could be very nasty indeed during the heyday of empire when the shackles of morality had been successfully cast off. But it wasn't just the murderous comic interludes at the local amphitheatre that tickled the Roman fancy. Laughter was an indulgence that went hand-in-hand with eating and drinking, and rich folk often hired, or even employed full-time, clowns, mimes or jesters to liven up their dinner parties. A lot of the humour turned on scurrilous impersonations of well-known figures, or the acting out of absurd scenes. The historian Mary Beard, in her wonderful book *Laughter in Ancient Rome*, calls mime one of the key institutions of Roman laughter. It was not, she says, mime as we understand it, but a partly scripted and partly improvised performance with dialogue and song, which featured both male and female actors. Mime could be so bawdy that some people refused to allow it at their banquets.

The *copreae*, or 'little shits', were professional entertainers that only the most prestigious householders could afford to employ. Before he became emperor, the socially inept Claudius was often the butt of their pranks. When he fell asleep at parties, for example, they would put ladies' slippers on his hands so that he rubbed his face with them when he awoke. Apparently this was thought funny enough to justify the *copreaes'* exorbitant fees.

Fools rule
In the Middle Ages, if you wanted to stay out of trouble, you kept your head down and toed the line. You stuck with the group,

you knew your place and, if you had any personal ambitions, it was best not to let on. This was a time of great moral and material insecurity. The Church ruled with an iron fist. As the supreme expression of non-conformist individuality, silliness of any kind represented a potentially dangerous break with social convention that had to be kept firmly in check.

Not that the Middle Ages were humourless. Far from it. Life was hard, but that was all the more reason to occasionally let off steam with a spot of mockery, a bawdy song or a dirty joke, many of which we know about because monks in their monasteries dutifully recorded them. Early Christian scholars could be remarkably open-minded. It's easy to imagine them chuckling away to themselves as they peppered their manuscripts with playful and subversive marginalia depicting mischievous monkeys, musical donkeys, arse-licking priests and tumbling acrobats. Rabbits lop off people's heads, carry dogs around in baskets, and do unspeakable things to damsels and comely young men. One fourteenth-century doodle shows a jousting match between a dog riding a rabbit and a rabbit on the back of a snail-man. Why so many rabbits and snails? Nobody seems to know. Perhaps they were the creatures the monks most often came into contact with as they tilled the monastery gardens.

The trick, for the authorities, was to ensure that frivolities remained on the margins, while the main business of life was conducted with appropriate solemnity. Nobody could be in any doubt about when nonsense was acceptable and when it was not.

That most marginalised group of all, the physically deformed, were always good for a laugh. If you were a dwarf, or had some kind of facial abnormality, a hunched back or crippled legs, your prospects in life were not good, but getting yourself employed as a fool in an aristocratic household or, at the very least, attaching yourself to a group of travelling entertainers, might allow you to survive as a 'licensed fool'. It was not necessary to be disabled, of course, but mental alertness was essential. Fools were not mad, but intelligent, rational people playing at being mad. They needed to be literate and able to memorise stories and poems, acting them out with gusto, adapting them to the situation and keeping them topical. They might also have been called on to play the lute, sing, dance, juggle, do magic tricks, or to fart melodically and whistle at the same time – a skill that Roland the Farter perfected to wow them at the court of Henry II in the twelfth century. Of course, they had to be able to make fun of their own deformity, if they had one, while maintaining the knife-edge balance between ridiculing and flattering hosts and guests. Since they were entirely at the mercy of their superiors, the consequences of overstepping the mark could mean a whipping or worse.

Quick-witted fools could become valuable properties, enjoying high status and protection from enemies at court (since not everyone enjoyed being the butt of their insolence). John Scoggin, for example, was said to be an Oxford-educated scholar, well versed in philosophy and the sciences, who spent the greater part of his life living in comfort as the favourite fool of Edward IV in the 1400s. *Scoggin's Jests, Full of Witty Mirth and Pleasant Shifts* ..., a collection of his rather dubious pranks, was a bestseller. One of his most inventive tricks was also one of the simplest: before introducing his wife to the queen, he told each woman, in strictest confidence, that the other was stone-deaf.

That so embarrassed the queen it got him temporarily banished from court.

The prospects for 'Natural fools', meaning the mentally disabled, were not so bright. Most were reduced to begging or entertaining passers-by on street corners for spare coins. Those whose madness took a melancholy turn had little choice but to throw themselves on the mercy of the Church, which must have cheered them up no end.

Thus, for one tiny group of people during the Middle Ages and Renaissance, the ability to be silly might mean the difference between life and death. Jesters and fools were an indispensable part of European court life, which was otherwise not flush with entertainments. Their fortunes, as the historian Beatrice Otto explains, 'rose and fell with the tsunami-scale wave of medieval and Renaissance fool mania that engulfed the Continent. The concept of folly with all its variegated hues permeated Europe at all levels for several centuries, and it is against this backdrop of colourful and often contradictory manifestations of "folly" that the European jester must be seen. There were certainly jesters before the tidal wave began to swell, but it is on its crest that we see them come surfing in'.[7]

The execution of Charles I in 1649 brought this happy state of affairs to an abrupt end, in England at least. The Puritans could not tolerate enjoyment of any kind. As theatres and taverns were shut down, actors joined fools, jesters and other fun-lovers in an exodus to Ireland and the Continent. In France, it was not until the Revolution that they got the chop (metaphorically speaking), the Jacobins having no more sense of humour than the Puritans. Political revolutionaries are rarely fun guys.

Jesters were not just a European phenomenon. They had

a major impact on Chinese court life right up until the early twentieth century and, for some emperors, it would have been unthinkable to make important decisions without first consulting their favourite fools. Beatrice Otto's book provides an exhaustive account. When Cortéz bullied his way into the court of Montezuma in 1520, he discovered the Aztec ruler surrounded by a retinue of jesters, who appeared to enjoy more power than he did (although appearances were deceptive, of course). Nor was it just court-life that needed the frisson of comic contrariness, many tribal societies had their revered pranksters as well. Native American tribes fostered some remarkably nonsensical behaviour from an assortment of holy fools.

If you didn't have actual, flesh-and-blood fools to leaven your toils – or even if you did – you could always invent some. The archetypal Trickster, who features in one form or another in folk tales the world over, uses his wit and intelligence to ensure that human life is never predictable. Trickster is usually male, although he might turn into a woman or an animal when it suits him. He has the mentality of an infant, and can be just as infuriating. One minute he's cheating people out of their possessions and throwing their lives into disarray, the next he's recovering lost children or even helping with the housework. He is the opposite of order, which makes him both a convenient scapegoat when things go wrong and a guilt-free explanation for good fortune. Just like the real-life fool or jester, the trickster is a go-between: a halfway figure, hovering between normality and madness, conformity and anarchy, the observable world and the unknown. He is an amoral outsider who can reconcile differences.

If a girl fell pregnant in the south-western United States, for example, it was because the trickster Kokopelli had left his gigantic detachable penis lurking in the river where she bathed, a prospect no doubt both terrifying and (in the sense that it absolved the young couple of responsibility) reassuring. When Brazilian farm animals escaped, or the milk turned sour or, really, when anything around the house went awry, it was because Saci, the one-legged dwarf with the magic hat, had been up to his old tricks again. For the Maui, the day was just the right length because Kappa, the God of a Thousand Tricks, had used his grandmother's magic jawbone to beat the Sun God (although Kappa's interventions were not always so helpful). And, as everyone knew, an Irish woman with tired feet had been dancing the night away with leprechauns.

Today we have our own version of Trickster in the form of Bugs Bunny, even if we can't believe in him in quite the same way.

Madness as a warning

Jesters and tricksters are the natural ancestors of modern nonsense. They kept alive, through the grimmest times, the idea that humour, especially when intended solely to raise a laugh, is an essential part of being alive: the salt that adds zest to life's banquet.

Meanwhile, the common folk were making their own fun – at least when the authorities and the pressures of daily life allowed. All over the world, wherever people have gathered together to let off steam, from the ancient Roman Saturnalia to Woodstock, religious or secular authorities have rushed either to institutionalise their misbehaviour (often in the hope of profiting from it) or try to stamp it out altogether. Few things are more vexing to those in power than the masses having a good time unsupervised.

So, the temporary setting aside of normal social behaviour during Carnival had its nefarious purpose. It was an object lesson for the common folk about what life would be like without rules. However much fun it was for a week or two, you wouldn't want to live that way all the time. The madness of Carnival was a warning.

The dilemma is nicely visualised in Pieter Bruegel the Elder's painting, *The Battle Between Carnival and Lent* (1559). It catches an important turning point in the medieval calendar when the drunken excesses of Carnival, with its music, feasting and play, give way to the grim self-denial of Lent. It is one of Bruegel's chaotically busy scenes, crowded with more than 200 figures and alive with incident and anecdote.

From a high vantage point we look down on a busy town square, where a ritualised battle is being fought between a gaunt Lady Lent and a fat King Carnival. Lady Lent's followers, spilling from an imposing church, are a pious lot: black-clad parishioners fresh from prayers, children spinning tops and a respectable-looking burgher with prayer book in hand, ostentatiously distributing alms. Whether high class or low, these folk are respectful, orderly and morally upright – and, Bruegel subtly suggests, not without hypocrisy.

On the other side of the square, outside a tavern, a fat butcher – king for the day – straddles a barrel. He faces his adversary with a pork chop on a pike and a large pie on his head, while a woman follows bearing bread and waffles. Behind them, drunken revellers cheer a group of travelling performers, musicians play, vendors sell their wares, beggars solicit alms and a pig roots happily in the dirt.

So which does Bruegel favour, festivity or religious observance? It's hard to tell. He probably felt, along with most others at the time, that an end to the good times was inevitable, that Carnival and Lent were two sides of the same coin. It's easy to get sentimental about medieval Carnival. Bruegel makes it look so jolly. It's all very well looking down at it from his high vantage point, especially at this distance in time, but a closer examination of his crowded scene reveals its violence and lawlessness. Were you to find yourself amid the scrum, being robbed, sexually assaulted or set upon by a drunken mob, you might have been inclined to side with the authorities.

By including a young married couple by a well in the middle of his picture, Bruegel suggests that out of the extreme debauchery of Carnival and the extreme self-denial of Lent a satisfying middle ground might be found. Today, that looks like wishful thinking. Carnival's insistent bracketing-off of pleasure, as if it were something to be got out of the way so the serious business of living and worshipping could continue undisturbed, sends a pretty clear message that real life is not meant to be fun.

Wise rulers who want to maintain order will encourage some occasional role-playing among their subjects. It must be strictly controlled, of course, and for a limited time. The peasants can let their hair down, dress in fancy costumes and prance around pretending to be kings or queens or lawmakers. It's all in good fun and, if the real king and queen suffer a few insults, that will quickly be forgotten when everything returns to normal. Inversion rituals are common all over the world. But they work only so long as the powerful feel secure. Once the lower orders start taking the message to heart (once they realise that their lowly status may not be pre-ordained by God after all), and once they detect signs of weakness or vulnerability among their betters, things might start getting tense. It's not hard to foresee that some malcontents might start thinking to themselves, 'If we can mock the clergy and usurp our rulers during Carnival, why can't we do it all the time? Why can't we overthrow the existing order for real?' There were those who took Carnival not as a warning but an invitation.

The panicked response of the Church in the seventeenth century was to shut down all forms of public expression, just to be on the safe side. Sporting events, fairs, public feasting and drinking, unauthorised processions and wakes came under attack all across Europe. Any outburst of riotous behaviour, or indeed any suggestion of public assembly, was met with violent repression. In *Dancing in the Streets*, her 'history of collective joy', Barbara Ehrenreich goes so far as to claim that Europe in the seventeenth century was plunged into what looks to us today like 'an epidemic of depression', affecting young and old alike.

As a result, fun and games went underground, replaced by morbid lassitude and fear. People abandoned the public squares, gathering instead in taverns, houses and halls, where they were more likely to be spectators of events prepared for them by others than participants in their own. They became consumers of fun instead of producers. And so we remain today, albeit for different reasons.

One advantage was that people gathering in small groups could tailor their fun to their own tastes, free from the dictates of the mob. So, when the mood finally lightened in the eighteenth century, a refined Englishman, with wife or mistress in tow, could enjoy one of dozens of new theatres, safely separated from the booing and fruit-throwing lower classes in the stalls. Or he could stroll with his companions in a pleasure garden, enjoying the flowerbeds, fountains, music and acrobats. For the less discriminating, Toby the Performing Pig at the local assembly rooms, or Mrs Bark, the seven-foot giantess (actually a shaven bear in a dress) might be just the ticket. And if, at the rougher end of the social spectrum, cockfighting or bull baiting proved a bit tame for jaded appetites, there was no shortage of public executions to provide an enjoyable day out for the family.

Meanwhile, across southern Europe, everyone turned out when the *commedia dell'arte* troupe rolled raucously into town. Their gaudy caravans brought singing, dancing, puppetry and colourful costumes, not to mention the sheer novelty of exotic strangers from the outside world. Hovering in the air was a scintillating aura of danger, since everyone knew what sort of people travelling performers were. For peasants, artisans, domestic servants and children of all classes, the arrival of these free spirits provided a thrilling glimpse of the larger world beyond their ken. It's no wonder that *commedia dell'arte* was the dominant form of commercial theatre in Europe from the mid-sixteenth to the mid-eighteenth centuries.

The storylines, straight out of Plautus, were simple and predictable: typically two lovers overcoming obstacles, usually in the form of disapproving elders, to find everlasting happiness in each other's arms. You could tell who was who – the wicked stepmother, the devious servant, the miser, the bully and so on – by the vividly painted masks the actors were wearing. Because the dialogue was mostly improvised, there was plenty of scope for nonsense and ribaldry and it was the edgy combination of predictability and seat-of-the-pants inventiveness that made it so much fun. In any case, the profusion of local dialects meant that many in the audience couldn't understand a word. They were there to enjoy the slapstick. Even so, there was plenty for them to identify with, such as the poor man who is so hungry he eats himself, or the helpful male servant who revives his haughty mistress when she faints by pissing on her. It was pretty basic stuff, but gloriously cathartic.

It wasn't much of a leap to dispense with dialogue altogether. Pantomime used stock characters – Arlecchino (or Harlequin), the scheming servant; Colombina, the mistress's companion; Scaramuccia (originally the 'killer of Moors'); Pantalone, the lecherous miser; and the long-nosed Pulcinella – to act out the familiar stories by means of gesture, dance and music. As in the *commedia*, little if anything was written down, the actors, sometimes with puppets, deftly weaving their own interpretations around the well-known plots as they went along, keeping things topical and popping in the occasional local reference. For the audience, it had the benefit of being comfortingly familiar yet new at the same time. And, of course, riotously funny. Like *commedia*, there was an awful lot of whacking, pushing, kicking, tripping, falling over and rudely gesturing.

After the Restoration of 1660, the English came up with their own much broader version of pantomime, a kind of musical-comedy stage show suitable for the whole family with songs, jokes, pacey dialogue, and lots of opportunities for audience participation. Pulcinella, originally a complex mixture of cunning trickster and low-life boor, and thus the embodiment of Neapolitan verve, morphed into the aptly named Punch, a compulsive beater of his long-suffering wife, Judy. Their descendants are dutifully doing the rounds of country fairs to this day under the guise of cultural heritage, although with the domestic violence tactfully suppressed.

Rabelaisian

Silliness ebbs and flows like the seasons. Some eras nurture it in warm, fertile ground, while at other times, when wintry seriousness or melancholy reign, it is left to struggle against the odds. It is not only during periods of freedom and relaxation that silliness is able to flower: this is a hardy specimen and political and religious oppression can sometimes give it just the frisson it needs. As a general rule, however, a degree of material wellbeing, political stability, intellectual freedom and social confidence provide the ideal growing conditions.

If the European sixteenth century, the era of court jesters, pantomime and Carnival, was a high-water mark, then its guiding spirit was François Rabelais, an older contemporary of Peter Bruegel the Elder. 'Nothing could be more playful than Rabelais,' declares the great theorist of play, Johan Huizinga. 'He is the play-spirit incarnate.'

Posterity has conferred on him the highest honour an author can achieve: it has turned him into an adjective. 'Rabelaisian' is defined by the Oxford Dictionary as 'an exuberance of imagination and language, combined with extravagance and coarseness of humour and satire', which sums him up perfectly. While *The Life and Opinions of Tristram Shandy, Gentleman* will strike many modern readers as long-winded and archaic, and

Don Quixote (dare I say it) tedious, Rabelais's *Gargantua and Pantagruel*, in a lively translation, remain as fresh as a baker's fart (although there is a version on the internet full of 'thee's and 'thou's and 'hitherto's, which manages to make heavy going of it). These five books, first published between 1535 and 1564, are, like *Don Quixote*, essentially satires on popular hero myths, but they veer off at every opportunity into exuberant madness. Pantagruel is a foul-mouthed giant who can vanquish any enemy and outwit any opponent, by trickery, charm, violence or subterfuge. His father, Gargantua, formerly a mild-mannered scholar, has been driven mad by his teachers and now harbours dreams of world domination, although he does soften with age. Pantagruel's inseparable companion Panurge is 'a felon, a cheat, a tippler, a loafer, a scrounger, but that apart, the nicest young lad in the world'.[8] Their preposterous adventures unfold in a whirlwind of twisted logic, dazzling wordplay, and some devastating satirical swipes, with much shitting, pissing, farting and fucking along the way.

Theirs is very much a man's world: shockingly so to modern sensibilities, but Rabelais was a product of his time. Women, when they do get a look in, are invariably the subjects of male sexual aggression or the hapless victims of childbirth. During the interminable debate in the third book about whether Panurge should marry, the prospective brides' opinions never get a look-in. And the only time Pantagruel's mother is mentioned is when she dies giving birth to him: not surprisingly, since 'there first sallied forth from her belly sixty-eight muleteers, each leading by the halter a mule laden with salt; after which came nine dromedaries laden with smoked bacon and ox-tongues, seven camels with eels, and then five-and-twenty wagons with leeks, garlic, chibols and onions'.

The attending midwives are unfazed, merely noting with satisfaction that they will all be well stocked for a while. Finally, 'out comes Pantagruel, all over hair like a bear. In a spirit of prophecy one of the sage-women declares: "Born hairy was he! Wondrous deeds will he do!" ...'[9] As indeed he does.

What's remarkable about Rabelais is that, unlike his heirs James Joyce and Samuel Beckett, a love of jokes, wordplay and fantasy doesn't preclude a warm and genuine interest in people. His characters are real, they live on the page and their personalities change and develop. Against all the odds, he manages to make Pantagruel and his companions likeable – even loveable – which, given their appalling behaviour, is quite an authorial feat.

Rabelais was an eminent physician and a student of law, blessed with limitless curiosity and an innate love for humanity. He immersed himself in the world of student farces, bawdy popular songs and street banter. He drew on medieval joke books, such as those of John Scoggin, but was equally well-versed in the classics. He freely stole from all his sources, he borrowed, adapted, subverted and mixed them together to weave intricate webs of absurdity. And his laughter rings down the centuries to this day.

A surfeit of logic

It's paradoxical that the next great flowering of silliness, a couple of centuries later, was nourished by the Enlightenment, the Age of Reason. But not as paradoxical as it seems, for reason and silliness go together like eating and shitting. The eighteenth century was an exciting time to be alive, provided, of course, you had some money and an inquiring mind. For the very first time, reading, writing, journalism and book publishing began to expand into the public sphere. In coffee houses, clubs and academies, discussion of ideas flourished, free from the threat of persecution.

It was only natural that clever, mischievous people, familiar with the discourse of the times, would take delight in seeing what devilry they could get up to, what boundaries of sense and decorum they might poke a disruptive stick at. They were greatly assisted by lax libel and copyright laws. In the eighteenth century, you could get away with insults and calumnies that would be unthinkable today. Take, for example, the curious practice of publishing bootleg copies of learned books, identical to the originals except for the insertion of scurrilous footnotes and absurdly misleading indexes. The unwary reader might be well into the text before waking up to the scam.

As that example suggests, these wags – writers and journalists in the main – were not anti-Enlightenment, let alone anti-intellectual, since they took full advantage of the freedoms the age had granted them and were familiar with the philosophical and literary ideas they were subverting. All the same, the intellectual fashion for disruptive nonsense was clearly a rebuff to the simplistic idea that everything was, in the final analysis, subject to reason. A surfeit of logic is always a happy breeding ground for the illogical.

And few books are more determinedly illogical – or anti-logical – than that compendium of pointless irrelevancies, Laurence Sterne's *Tristram Shandy*. I tried reading it for the first time when I was young and gave up, not because it was beyond my understanding, but because I could not reconcile myself to the fact that something so sophisticatedly 'modern' had been written more than 250 years earlier. It upset all my preconceptions about the past. Laurence Sterne's anarchic cock-and-bull story tells us almost nothing of the hero's life or opinions, not even getting around to his birth until nearly halfway through. Then, having finally come into the world, the hero fades away and the book, which never really managed to get started, is hijacked by a host of minor characters. The narrative, peppered with pranks and jests, is constantly interrupted by lengthy – sometimes insanely lengthy – digressions.

For instance, Chapter 21 of Volume I begins innocently enough with Tristram's father complaining to Uncle Toby about the racket upstairs:

> I wonder what's all that noise, and running backwards and forwards for, above stairs, quoth my father, addressing himself, after an hour and a half's silence, to my uncle Toby, — who you must know, was sitting on the opposite side of the fire, smoking his social pipe all the time, in mute contemplation of a new pair of black-plush-breeches which he had got on; —What can they be doing, brother? — quoth my father, —we can scarce hear ourselves talk.
>
> I think, replied my uncle Toby, taking his pipe from his mouth, and striking the head of it two or three times upon the nail of his left thumb, as he began his sentence, — I think, says he: —But to enter rightly into my uncle Toby's sentiments upon this matter, you must be made to enter a little into his character, the outlines of which I shall just give you, and then the dialogue between him and my father will go on as well again.[10]

It is only eleven chapters later, well into Volume II, that the dialogue is allowed to continue and we discover that the noise upstairs is Mrs Shandy going into labour. It's been a very long hiatus. *Tristram Shandy*, published in instalments between 1759 and 1766, was immensely popular in England and France and made its author famous. It was, contrary to my youthful prejudices, in perfect harmony with the sophisticated tastes of the time. The eighteenth century was a golden age for wordplay, ridicule, derision, joking and bawdiness, in books and pamphlets, theatrical performances, journalism and popular songs and ditties. Sterne's extraordinary book encapsulates its times.

One hundred per cent pure

Then, during the course of the nineteenth century, God died, and the fun times seemed to die with Him. He had not been looking well for some time before Friedrich Nietzsche officially declared Him dead in 1882. Darwin's *On the Origin of Species* and *The Descent of Man* had earlier raised the alarming prospect that, far from being the apples in God's eye, human beings were mere accidents of nature in a universe without purpose or meaning. As if people didn't have enough to worry about.

Nietzsche, while not unaware of the moral dangers, also saw the positive side, rejoicing at finding himself in a freer, less guilt-ridden world (although he was hardly what you'd call a light-hearted chap). A universe without purpose or meaning, while it might be terrifying, is, he helpfully pointed out, one of endless possibilities.

Sadly, though, most nineteenth-century thinkers chose not to take the Nietzschean option. There was an awful lot of metaphorical wrist slitting. This was, on the whole, an era of high seriousness, much given to melancholy of a very self-important kind (with Wagner its ponderous epitome). We see little of the bawdy love of life of a century earlier.

Even the comic absurdities of Gogol – the man's nose that detaches itself from his face and goes off to seek a better life, or the man who imagines he is the king of Spain and surreptitiously reads the correspondence between two dogs – turn, as a contemporary critic put it, 'into a Holbein-like dance of death'. The typical Gogolian character is a nobody, desperately and unsuccessfully trying to assert himself against a wall of indifference. The main character of 'The Overcoat', a humble office clerk, is compared to a dead fly pinned to a card under a microscope, dear to nobody and undistinguished.

Gogol's is silliness of a unique kind: certainly not the kind Rabelais or Sterne would have recognised. He co-opts it as a way of coping with anxiety, something that would have a huge influence on the bleak, nihilistic nonsense of twentieth-century writers such as Beckett, Joyce and Ionesco. A deeply religious man, Gogol wanted to demonstrate that, in the absence of God, nothing can make sense. All the same, 'a Holbein-like dance of death' might be going a bit far. There is a lot of life in Gogol's characters, for all their subjection, and his sentences fizz with expectation. For where there's absurdity, there's hope.

On the whole, however, silliness at this very serious time was not considered an adult affair, being quite beneath the dignity of grown-ups. Not that this was entirely a bad thing, because it freed the way to pure literary silliness, unhitched from satire.

The Reverend Charles Dodgson, Gogol's older contemporary, was a pious Deacon of Christ Church, Oxford, where he taught mathematics and logic. Although inquisitive and open to ideas, he was socially conservative and never wavered in his Christian faith. Dodgson's alter ego, Lewis Carroll, is a different person altogether: outward-looking, non-judgemental and free-spirited. The Alice books have no moral to push and reveal virtually nothing of their author's social or political views. Carroll shows no anxiety about the death of God, instead creating an alternative world in which it doesn't figure. His books are delightful nonsense which, although they have subsequently spawned a great deal of social and psychological interpretation, carry no messages.

All literary silliness up until this point had been wrapped in a cloak of satire. However outrageous and bizarre Aristophanes, Rabelais or Sterne may be, their overriding intention is to hold contemporary standards of behaviour up to ridicule. Theirs is, to quote G.K. Chesterton, 'a kind of exuberant capering round a discovered truth'. Carroll, and his compatriot, the poet Edward Lear, are content with exuberant capering purely for the sake of a good caper. Consider, for example, the opening verse of Lear's *The Pobble who has no Toes*:

> *The Pobble who has no toes*
> *Had once as many as we;*
> *When they said 'Some day you may lose them all,'*
> *He replied 'Fish, fiddle-de-dee!'*
> *And his Aunt Jobiska made him drink*
> *Lavender water tinged with pink,*
> *For she said 'The World in general knows*
> *There's nothing so good for a Pobble's toes!'*

This is not a critique of anything: it is off in a delightful world of its own. Carroll and Lear put into writing what popular songs and nursery rhymes had been saying for centuries: that laughter and play are all you need, provided you're a child, of course.

Chesterton (not exactly a neutral observer when it comes to matters of religion) wryly observed that even Lear's nonsense might have a religious implication because it reawakens the sense of wonder upon which religious experience hinges, and which Chesterton feared materialism was destroying. Nonsense, he says, engenders a proper appreciation of 'the huge and undecipherable unreason' of creation and therefore serves as a parallel to faith. It's a nice conceit, but I wonder if he's taking it all a bit too seriously.

Laughter in the dark

In Richard Attenborough's 1969 film of *Oh! What a Lovely War*, General Douglas Haig is shown cavorting happily with a group of officers and their wives on Brighton Pier while, behind them, a cricket scoreboard records the latest casualties: '1915/ BATTLE OF LOOS/ BRITISH LOSSES – 60,000/ TOTAL ALLIED LOSSES – 250,000/ GROUND GAINED – 0 YARDS'. And to think that World War I had started out so well.

No rational response would do in the face of such mind-numbing statistics. The utter insanity of war had crushed the old order and reduced everything to meaninglessness. European civilisation was teetering on the edge of an abyss and there was only one possible course of action: to sneak up behind it and give it a push.

In 1916, a group of writers and artists coalesced in Zurich around the mercurial Romanian poet Tristan Tzara. Their 'soirées' involved anarchic debates on nonsensical subjects, ad-hoc theatrical performances, loud declamations of nonsense poetry accompanied by whistles, bangs and shouts, and exhibitions of 'anti-art'. Dada was born. It was, according to Hugo Ball, who like many in the movement was a refugee from the fighting, 'a public execution of false morality'. Dada was motivated by disgust. It ushered in something that would become a feature of the terrible twentieth century: silliness that had no intention of being funny.

For the Dadaists, art had no sense or meaning, no moral or material worth. The freedom they sought was not just freedom from bourgeois values, as is often supposed, but from rationality itself. Artworks were made by randomly tearing things up, rubbing chalk across a rough surface or pressing paper onto spilt ink. Poetry was cobbled together from words randomly pulled from a hat. Music might be the noise of machinery, or people shouting or banging frenetically on tin cans.

The German artist Kurt Schwitters's Merz pictures (the name, suitably enough, is meaningless), which he began making towards the end of the war, are seemingly random assemblages of objects glued, screwed or nailed onto flat surfaces. Sweet wrappers, lace doilies, scraps of advertising, pieces of wood, random words and even bicycle parts happily rub shoulders in casual defiance of every principle of picture-making. They were a rude shock to contemporary audiences, although they will strike most of us today as rather beautiful and suspiciously well-designed (and, although Schwitters died in poverty, they sell for millions).

Where to after Dada? Intellectually, it was a bit of a dead end. All the same, its indirect influence was immense. The disgust that had been its original motivation developed (or should that be 'descended') into political satire of an increasingly savage kind; its forays into the irrational drifted inexorably into the solipsistic romanticism of Surrealism; and its childishness found a home in absurdist comedy, which to my mind (although I admit to being biased), is Dada's most enduring legacy.

Silliness at sixteen frames a second

The story goes that, when the Lumière Brothers' short film of a train arriving at La Ciotat station was first screened in 1896, people screamed and ducked for cover, thinking the huge locomotive was going to run right over them. Looking at this innocuous little snippet now, we might find that hard to believe, but true or not, the anecdote is a potent reminder of the power and immediacy of the moving image. Even today, given wide-screen projection, 3D, Dolby Surround and loads of sophisticated CGI, we might still be able to recapture some of that sense of wonder.

While the Lumières concentrated on recording day-to-day life in Parisian streets, satisfied that the very act of recording a moving image was extraordinary enough in its own right, Georges Méliès, a professional magician, was quick to realise cinema's potential for fantasy and play. Méliès is cinema's first storyteller, and arguably still its greatest illusionist. In more than 200 short films, each one a delightful excursion into a world of crazy make-believe, he gave turn-of-the-century audiences an enchanting alternative to the materialism of the age.

He films himself using a giant bellows to inflate his head until it explodes. He keeps removing his head from his shoulders, a new one springing up each time to replace it, while the severed heads chatter gaily to one another on a table in front of him. In *The Untameable Whiskers* of 1904, we watch as a man's facial hair gets seriously out of control. Méliès' most famous film, *A Trip to the Moon* (1902), is a riot of anti-scientific and anti-rational mumbo-jumbo. A group of bumbling astronomers climb into a homemade rocket, which is manoeuvred into the barrel of a giant cannon by a bevy of pixies. A moment later, it strikes the man-in-the-moon squarely in the eye, wiping the manic grin off his face. After getting caught in a snowstorm, lost in a cave of giant mushrooms, and being attacked by angry moon-men, the astronauts hurry back to their rocket, push it over the edge of a cliff and fall directly back down to earth.

Méliès' considerable technical achievements, which dazzled audiences of a century or more ago, inevitably look dated today. But really, who cares? His extraordinary imagination, wit and exuberance, and his Rabelaisian love of play are still capable of bringing us joy.

While more sophisticated cameras, lighting and editing equipment allowed the Keystone cops, Charlie Chaplin and Buster Keaton to create ever-more elaborate sight-gags, topping Méliès' quirky resourcefulness was a taller order. He paved the way for the great American comedians of the pre-talkies era, a fact acknowledged when he was dubbed a Knight of the Legion of Honour in 1931.

Today, we have the internet to give us instant access to all this riotous creativity. From Aristophanes to Woody Allen, it's all there at the click of a mouse (or is that already an outdated reference?). What's extraordinary is how quickly we have come to take this unparalleled superabundance for granted.

Silliness: A Serious History

In my twenties, I hitchhiked from Melbourne to Adelaide for a screening of *A Trip to the Moon*. I thought it might be the only chance I'd ever get to see it. Today I can watch it, along with over a hundred of Méliès's other films, on my phone while waiting for a bus.

Yet, more than just turning us into uber-consumers, the internet gives us an uncensored and non-discriminating platform. If your dog's bum looks like Jesus, if you've just filmed your sister falling face forward into her wedding cake, if you've been lucky enough to be behind a hippopotamus with diarrhoea, or if you've written an hilarious piece about teaching ravens to fly underwater (Peter Cook got in before you with that one, of course, but fortunately originality is not an issue any more), your audience need no longer be limited to your long-suffering family and friends. It is not at all unusual for a video of some fool on a skateboard spectacularly failing to leap over a speeding car to be seen by hundreds of thousands of people. Not since 'fool mania' in the sixteenth century has silliness been so open to all comers. The internet might well be ushering in the greatest age of silliness yet.

The two faces of silliness

A Scottish boy I knew in high school told me that when he asked what haggis was, his mother, worried that he might turn up his nose if he knew, told him a story. The haggis, she said, was a small, furry animal that lived in the highlands where it had evolved with the legs on its right side twice the length of those on its left, allowing it to keep upright on the steep slopes. Sadly, this meant it couldn't turn around, so, having flushed it from its burrow, all you had to do was head off in the opposite direction and meet it head-on as it came around the other side of the mountain. Haggis was plentiful because it was so easy to catch. Even as a small child, my friend never really believed this, but he was happy to accept it because it was such a good story that the truth could only be a disappointment. Tall tales of this kind cemented the bond of complicity between mother and son.

But where do they come from? Who knows? They are handed down from generation to generation, or they are made up on the run by parents who either have no answer to their children's questions or, like the mother of my Scottish friend, have reason not to reveal it. They are part of the rich folk tradition of silliness, along with rhymes, riddles, songs and old-wives tales, retold and reinvented *ad infinitum* in schoolyards, taverns, workshops and domestic kitchens the world over. It is a tradition as old as language itself.

Cows that jump over the moon and cats that play the bagpipes, intolerable in any other setting, are part of the landscape of children's rhymes, and Kokopelli's giant detachable penis lurking in a river is an inventive and playful explanation for your daughter's pregnancy if you don't know about, or don't want to acknowledge, the alternative.

From the Ancient Roman *copreae*, through medieval Carnival, fools and jesters, mythical tricksters, *commedia dell'arte* and circus clowns, to flash mobs, flashers at the footy, and 'People Falling Over' on YouTube: these are the people's nonchalant up-yours to order, meaning and conformity.

Parallel to the folk tradition, although at one remove, is the more recent, and much better documented, literary tradition of silliness. Lewis Carroll and Edward Lear are usually credited with being its originators. They flattered their young readers by reflecting – and legitimising – a fantastic world that was already familiar to them. For adults, meanwhile, they highlighted the connection between childish nonsense and the burgeoning Victorian fascination with dreams and the irrational, thus, over time, bridging the gap between the generations.

Yet Carroll and Lear did not spring from nowhere. While the intentions of Aristophanes, Rabelais, Cervantes, Sterne and Gogol may have been broadly satirical, these authors revelled in nonsense and were capable of being flamboyantly and indulgently silly.

Someone once observed that if Cervantes or Rabelais were alive today, they would have little chance of winning the Nobel Prize. The Nobel is a serious prize awarded to *serious* literature (very few comic writers have won it: I think Dario Fo was the last). Perhaps we should be grateful. It confirms that humour – and silliness in particular – is still an irritant, still a thorn in the side of respectability.

Three TOO SILLY FOR WORDS

Nonsense words denote little or nothing while connoting a great deal. And the more they connote, the more delightful – or, as Roald Dahl might put it, the more phizz-whizzing – we are likely to find them. A word that has little or no specific meaning but encourages all kinds of creative associations is like a fuzzy core lit by a multi-coloured halo: a sprite, with no substance, nothing to take hold of, just an alluring, ever-shifting glow. Our delight springs from its suggestiveness, its cheeky provocation, its refusal to be pinned down. The nonsense word teases and beguiles, firing our imaginations as it takes us on a linguistic adventure with no clear goal in view.

Take 'brillig', for example, one of my favourite nonsense words. To me, this is a seasonal thing, connoting turned-up collars and frozen toes. Perhaps it has something to do with *brrrr*: the word itself sounds crisp and austere. Maybe I'm influenced by the next line in Lewis Carroll's famous poem, in which the slithy toves gyre and gimble in the wabe, which suggests furtive wriggling in some cold, damp place. Am I being too gloomy? Perhaps you are more optimistic, seeing brillig as a festival and the gyring and gimbling as gyrating and gambolling, in which case you'll be picturing a warm summer evening full of fairylights and joy (although that fails to account for 'slithy', doesn't it – that evocative mix of slimy and lithe). The point is, there is no right or wrong interpretation, that's what makes them such a treat, although the words themselves will offer a few pointers.

The one thing we will usually agree on, however, is their grammatical function. Even if we can't discern their meanings – in fact, even if we encounter them in isolation rather than as part of a sentence – we instinctively recognise 'brillig' as a noun, 'slithy' as an adjective, and 'gyre' and 'gimble' as either verbs or nouns. And we instinctively recognise this even if we're not too clear about what adjectives, nouns or verbs are. To appreciate the connotations of nonsense words, we need to be able to relate them to what we know. They must *seem* to make sense, to be apparently normal words with recognisable syntax, phonetics and forms.

In 2015, researchers at the University of Alberta devised an experiment to discover why some nonsense words are more amusing than others. It's not as subjective as you might think. It would be difficult to imagine anything less amusing than their dutifully academic report,[11] but it boils down to this: students were given lists of computer-generated nonsense words and asked to rank them according to how amusing they sounded. For reasons I don't quite understand, anything with a sexual connotation (or, as the researchers quaintly put it, anything 'rude'), such as cok, whong, clunt, dongl, was eliminated at the outset. As every schoolboy knows, a rude word in a non-rude context is always side-splittingly hilarious, so it was thought that this 'semantic complication', as they put it, would only mess with their meticulously calibrated results.

Unsurprisingly, words such as whook, strompa, bollyze,

quingel, probble and grappor were unanimously judged more amusing than mamessa, suppect, sectori or tessina. But why? The researchers never really come to grips with this question, suggesting that 'they violate our expectations of what a word is' (after Schopenhauer's Incongruity Theory). But they all do that, whether amusing or not. While, admittedly, their conclusions are a bit more comprehensive than this, none is satisfying. Maybe any attempt to explain why certain things tickle our fancy are bound to fall short. Despite the consistency of the Alberta study's results, which show a striking consensus about *which* nonsense words we find amusing, it's difficult to say definitively *why*, and perhaps we shouldn't even be trying.

But let's try anyway. Part of it, surely, is that nonsense words amuse us when they are onomatopoeic and suggestive: whook has whoosh or whack in it, grappor segues naturally into grab or groper. Furthermore, unlike the words that were judged unfunny – which are abstract, with few connotations – they are physical, even slapstick. As the Alberta researchers point out (citing the philosopher William James), 'Using a word is as much a matter of *feeling* as it is of thinking. Words don't just have different semantic and syntactic properties; they also *feel* different'.[12]

To see how much that feeling depends upon association, take this truly monstrous nonsense word from the beginning of *Finnegans Wake*: bababadalgharaghtakamminarronnkonnbronntonnerronntuonnthunntrovarrhounawnskawntoohoohoorde nenthurnuk. There's no way we can make anything of that! It's neither funny nor unfunny: just completely baffling, and it marks the point at which many readers will throw the book out the window. But when we discover that it represents the thunderclap that heralds the fall of Adam and Eve and combines words for thunder in several languages, it becomes intriguing, even rather endearing. Just the look of it on the page resembles an ominous rumbling along the horizon. So, it's not entirely gibberish, despite appearances. The caveat is that, although brillig, whook and grappor allow us lots of imaginative scope, Joyce's indigestible thunderclap depends on an explanation, and only one explanation will fit, so it leaves us with little to do besides admiring his cleverness.

Once upon a mpf

It's a wonderful word, 'gibberish', although nobody can quite agree where it comes from. We do know that it was first used in 1554, so it's been around for a while. Nor is it easy to settle on a definition. I tend to think of it not as a meaningless assemblage of existing words (that's either gobbledygook – a term coined as recently as 1944 by an American politician fed up with the language of bureaucrats – or mumbo jumbo). Gibberish is, instead, a string of made-up words with little or no intrinsic meaning.

There is an oddly effecting incident in the *Fourth Book of Pantagruel* in which the knockabout humour of the rest of the book softens into poetic melancholy. During their epic ocean voyage in search of the Oracle of the Holy Bottle, Pantagruel, Gargantua and Panurge are unnerved one morning by mysterious voices rising off the sea into the motionless air. These turn out to be the ghostly echoes of a nearby battle the previous winter, when the shouts and cries of soldiers, the cracks of cannon fire and all the din of war had instantly turned to ice. Now, as the ice melts, the sounds, held captive for so long, are gradually being released. Scooping the brightly coloured chunks of ice from the water, Pantagruel and his friends lay them on the deck to thaw so they can listen in to that long-ago conflict. Rabelais has chanced upon sound recording, some 350 years before it became a reality (although he 'borrowed' the idea from Plutarch, who, in turn, borrowed it from an even earlier writer). Yet what they hear, amongst a few bloodthirsty cries and curses, is gibberish: *hing, hing, hing, hing, hisse, hickory dickory dock, brededing, brededac, frr, frrr, frrr.* This unselective muddle of human cries, horses' neighs, cannon fire, bugles and drums is just the sort of thing you might expect if you played back a recording of any battle scene without the aid of visual clues. The past cannot be recaptured from this meaningless jumble of noises.

Unlike 'brillig', 'gyre' and 'gimble', which are suggestive and evocative, gibberish doesn't connote much, if anything. Nor do gibberish words usually admit to any grammatical function – it's difficult to tell whether they are meant to be nouns, verbs or adjectives. Not that it matters, because gibberish sentences don't usually have any grammatical structure, no subject, predicate or object. In other words, they are not likely to be sentences at all, but strings of apparently meaningless sounds, all of equal status.

In real life, gibberish is the preserve either of children, the insane, or the aged: that is, when rational adult behaviour is still under development or is slipping away. The infant's *ga-ga-ga-ga* is gibberish (or, technically, babbling) at its most fundamental, a futile striving for communication before the means become available. Glugly, a tall thin child in C.S. Lewis's *The Pilgrim's Regress*, entertains her friends with an awkward little dance, singing, 'Globol, obol, oogle oble globol gloo', then pursing her lips and making vulgar noises 'such as children make in their nurseries'. [13]

At the other end of life's journey, Clive James recalls his aged grandfather reading him bedtime stories, which the young Clive could not understand and did all he could to avoid, not because the stories were over his head but because Granddad's speech 'by that stage consisted almost entirely of impediments. "Once upon a mpf," he would intone, "there wah ngung mawg blf."' [14]

Along with the humour there is pathos, even a little cruelty, in both these anecdotes. Whatever enjoyment Glugly's friends derive from her performance is bound to be at her expense. Neither she nor James's grandfather are aware that they are making fools of themselves, although in each case the authors, who are taking a certain delight in their subjects' humiliation, are. They are turning an inability to communicate into a form of communication.

The Dadaists were very fond of gibberish, as befits a movement supposedly named after an infant's first utterance. They were not the first poets to produce what one linguist has clumsily called 'alogical amalgamations of unrelated vocables'. The German poet, Paul Scheerbart's *Kikakokù! Ekoraláps!* of 1897 is generally credited with being the earliest purely phonetic poem, although the French Symbolists were toying with similar notions at around the same time. The Futurists and Expressionists would later take up the cudgel in typically portentous style. But it was up to the Dadaists to make it fun – albeit savage fun. 'We renounce writing verse at second hand,' declared Hugo Ball, one of the movement's founders, 'that is, using words (let alone sentences) that we have not invented.' Ball's *Karawane* begins: 'jolifanto bambla o falli bambla/ großiga m'pfa habla horem'. He recited it at the Cabaret Voltaire in Zurich in 1916, wearing a mock-Cubist costume that made him look like a malevolent gnome and rendered movement all but impossible.

This sort of thing has its limitations, of course. The Austrian artist and writer, Raoul Hausmann, recalled a visit to the Alps with a group of his Dadaist colleagues, including Kurt Schwitters: 'The first thing that morning, Kurt began: "Fmsbwtäzäu, fmsbwtäzäu, pgiff, pgiff, mü ..." He did not stop all day ... On our way back, Schwitters again started on his "Fms, fms" and "fmsbw", it became a bit much'[15] (even for a fellow Dadaist). This was the birth of Schwitters' epic nonsense poem *Ursonate*, begun in 1923 and fiddled with for the next ten or so years. It was meant to be declaimed rather than read on the page and, according to one observer, Schwitters 'sang, trilled, whispered, snarled, shouted his *Ursonate* with overpowering élan, until the audience jumped out of their skins.' Presumably a few of them also jumped out of their seats and headed for the exit. On YouTube, you can hear Schwitters reciting a short extract from *Ursonate*. It probably won't make you jump out of your skin (not now, anyway, nearly a hundred years on, after decades of appalling uni reviews have inured us to this sort of thing) but it is affectingly lyrical, even rather beautiful, at times coming very close to birdsong.

Schwitters would go on to produce 'poems' that abandon words altogether, even made-up ones, consisting of nothing more than isolated letters of the alphabet. On the page, they could hardly be less interesting; the effect was all in the performance, which stretched the sounds beyond recognition.

Unlike the phonetic poetry of the Symbolists and Expressionists, Schwitters does not aspire to any extra-rational meaning or transcendent truth. He is just choreographing sounds for the pleasure of it, although he could not escape an undercurrent of regret. 'Everything had broken down in any case,' he said resignedly, 'and new things had to be made out of fragments.'[16]

It would take the Americans – specifically black Americans – to grab gibberish around the waist and get it onto the dance floor. At the Cotton Club in Harlem, at about the time Schwitters was intoning his *Ursonate*, they were jivin' to Cab Calloway, and having a lot more fun:

> When your sweetie tells you
> Everything'll be okay
> Just skeep-beep de bop-bop beep bop bo-dope
> Skeetle-at-de-op-de-day
> If you feel like shoutin'
> Advertise it just this way
> And skeep-beep de bop-bop beep bop bo-dope
> Skeetle-at-de-op-de-day

The folks at the Cotton Club had probably never heard of Dada, and neither, I assume, had Calloway. Having had little direct experience of the War to End all Wars, they probably didn't feel that everything had broken down. Not that they didn't have reason to complain, but they came to the Club to put their troubles behind them. Calloway was working in a tradition of freewheeling, improvised scat singing that went back to the turn of the century, although he made it distinctively his own.

The gibberish is always framed with coherent lyrics to keep it grounded. This makes it less adventurous, I suppose, than what the Dadaists were doing, but it reached a much bigger audience and was mercifully free of angst. This was gibberish you could get off on and some of its joyful spirit survives to this day in hip-hop.

Fiddle-de-dee

Treatises have been compiled about the educational value of nonsense words. They assist young people in learning about word construction and pronunciation and are especially useful in testing mental acuity. But, as far as the youngsters themselves are concerned, that's all bugwiffle. They're revelling in rhyme and rhythm and musicality, while eagerly anticipating the occasional hint of smut. They want a good giggle.

Even if they have no specific meaning, nonsense words are bound to reflect their times and their culture. They are not entirely unconnected to the world, although gibberish comes close. When we look back at nursery rhymes, stories and games from the seventeenth, eighteenth and nineteenth centuries, many of the nonsense words we find are borrowed from animals: the sort of noises that were a constant accompaniment to daily life. Animal noises intrigue us because, although they are clearly a form of vocal communication, they remain mostly indecipherable. They remind us of our separateness.

In the past, even most city children were on speaking terms with working animals. *The World of Things Obvious to the Senses*, written in the mid 1600s by John Comenius, is said to be the first book ever written specifically for children. Although it comprises a good deal of ponderous theology and philosophising, it begins in livelier fashion with a guide to animal sounds, aimed at helping young readers 'to speak out rightly'. 'The duck quacketh', 'the hare squeaketh' and the cat says 'nau-nau'. Having learned to imitate these sounds, Comenius rather grandly advises, 'we will go into the World, and we will view all things'.

There is an infectious vivacity to all the oinks, neighs, hee-haws and chickle-chackles that populate early children's literature, a real sense that these sounds meant something to young readers and mirrored their lived experience. When cows mooed, it really meant moo. In the subtlest of ways, the animal noises in poems, stories and songs reveal a tough-minded respect for, and an understanding of, non-human creatures which, even allowing for our sentimentality about the animals we find cuddly, is largely missing today.

Take, for example, the following awkward little rhyme, popular in the seventeenth century:

> *There was a lady loved a swine,*
> *'Honey', quoth she,*
> *'Pig-hog wilt thou be mine?'*
> *'Hoogh', quoth he.*[17]

There are several verses, all ending with the clumsy finality of 'Hoogh', which is splendidly pig-like and gives nothing away: if the pig is ready to make a commitment, he's being coy about it.

The duck that goes quack quack and the cow that goes moo moo in the well-known American folk song about a farm are nothing out of the ordinary. Along with oink oink, miaow miaow and woof woof, they are now so much a part of the language we hardly recognise them as made-up words at all. But the hen that goes chimmy-chuck, chimmy-chuck, the pig that goes griffy-gruffy and the cat that goes fiddle-de-dee are more inventive, being more than just onomatopoeic. Although fiddle-de-dee (or fiddle-i-fee as it's sometimes spelt) is not something a cat is likely to utter, it neatly encapsulates the feline's casual approach to life.

Fiddle-de-dee, with its jaunty musicality, crops up a lot in early ditties, usually in relation to cats. I'm not sure why, but it may have started with the best-known nonsense rhyme of all, which dates from the eighteenth century. Although almost everyone knows it by heart, it's worth reminding ourselves of just how gloriously silly and surreal it is:

> *Hey diddle diddle, the cat and the fiddle,*
> *The cow jumped over the moon.*
> *The little dog laughed to see such fun,*
> *And the dish ran away with the spoon.*

Today, although animals play a large part in children's literature and film, most of them are either pets, whose role is to flatter humans by reflecting their emotions, or humans in animal form, acting like people and talking like people, usually in American accents. In *The Lion King*, for example, the cubs not only engage in sophisticated banter but launch into disco numbers, with full orchestral backing. It's witty, erudite, frequently mawkish but, above all, ferociously anthropomorphic. Today, nonsense words, when they do occur in children's literature (and, Roald Dahl and Doctor Seuss aside, it's not all that often), are unlikely to take their cue from the utterances of pigs or sheep or horses, which are no longer a large part of a child's experience.

We all agree that horses say neigh. Or at least they do in English. Japanese horses say *hi-hin*, Russian horses *i-go-go* and Swedish horses *ihahaha*. French dogs say *ouah*, Greek dogs *gav* and Turkish dogs *hauv*. English pigs say oink, Hungarian pigs *rof*, Swedish pigs *nof* and Russian pigs *khryoo*. For some reason, though, almost all cats, regardless of where they live, say miaow, or some minor variation of it, except in Japan, where they prefer *nyan*. The sounds we hear from our animal companions are determined more by the language we speak than the language they speak. A British bulldog and a Siberian husky will have no trouble communicating.

A fascination with animal sounds is not just the preserve of children, however. Aristophanes liked nothing more than to dress up his actors as wasps or frogs or birds who, although quite capable of human language, occasionally lapsed into their own sound patterns just to remind us of who they really are. When the frog chorus first appears in *Frogs*, for instance, they sing:

> *Brekekekex, koax, koax,*
> *Brekekekex, koax, koax,*
> *Oh we are the musical Frogs!*
> *We live in the marshes and bogs!*
> *Sweet, sweet is the hymn*
> *We sing as we swim,*
> *And our voices are known*
> *For their musical tone ...*[18]

I have no idea what these frog calls sounded like in Attic Greek but, if David Barrett's translation is anything to go by, Aristophanes was admirably attentive to nature. This is just as I would expect a frog to sound and much more inventive than the usual croak or ribbit. The British author and traveller Patrick Leigh Fermor appears to agree: in his erudite memoir *A Time of Gifts*, he notes frogs brekekekexing in the forest.

In Aristophanes' *The Birds*, Epops, a former king, has been transformed into a hoopoe, a colourful crested bird still found today in Africa and Eurasia. '*Epo popo popo popo popo popo poi!*' he calls, '*Ió, ió, itó, itó, itó!*' You can listen to a hoopoe's call on YouTube and judge for yourself how accurate this is.

The now largely forgotten seventeenth-century poet John Taylor was, along with many of his contemporaries, scornful of efforts to civilise 'primitive' peoples through the glories of the English language. His *Epitaph in the Barmooda Tongue*, published in 1613, is written entirely in Barmoodan, a 'language' Taylor invented and which, he stated, 'must be pronounced with the accent of the grunting hogge'. The much-maligned hog is doomed to be the embodiment of crassness and ignorance. Taylor, who made his living as a Thames waterman ferrying passengers from one bank to the other, was party to many stories about the English voyages to the Americas. Clearly he was unimpressed, and the *Epitaph* is his contemptuous response to British cultural bullying. It begins: 'Hough gruntough wough Thomough Coriatough, Odcough robunquogh ...', every word ending with 'ough' or 'ogh'. The inclusion of an individual's name, the famous writer and traveller Thomas Coryat, confirms that the poem was more than gibberish but you'd have to be pretty keen to bother trying to decode it.

Like many so-called invented languages, Barmoodan is not really a language at all but merely a corruption of English. Its words are mangled English words, its grammar and syntax familiar. While Taylor's motivation is admirable, his protest fails in the execution. But at least he doesn't take himself too seriously: Barmoodan is his savage little joke.

Enriching the language

The translator of nonsense words has to be sensitive to what they suggest in the context of a sentence. Sound and rhythm are important, too, and how they might conform to or break the conventions of syntax and construction. It seems natural to assume that a word which doesn't mean anything in the original language won't need translating, but a made-up word that sounds funny or quirky in French could fall flat in English because it does not have the same connotations. M.A. Screech, translator of *Gargantua and Pantagruel*, had an additional problem. As well as inventing new words, Rabelais chopped and diced existing ones, then slotted them together in novel combinations. He also used foreign and obscure words that he knew would confound his readers. Screech had to find equivalents that would similarly confound – and amuse – modern English readers.

A perfect example comes early in book one. Pantagruel meets a dapper young student from Paris who is putting on the most outrageous airs. When Pantagruel innocently asks how students pass the time in Paris, he replies,

> We transfrete the Sequana at times dilucidatory and crepusculine, deambuating via the urbic carfaxes and quadrivia; we despumate the latinate verbocination, and, like verisimilitudinous amorevolous, we captivate the omnijudicious, omniform and omnigenous feminine sex.

> On certain dïes we invitate ourselves to the lupanars of Campgaillard, Matcon, Cul-de-sac, Bourbon and Huslieu [*these were famous brothels*]. There, in venereal ecstasy, we inculcate our veretra into the most absconce recesses of the pudenda of those more amicitial meretrices ...

He has learnt that to sound really authoritative, you must employ as many formal-sounding Latinate words as you can. Pantagruel puts up with a remarkable amount of this tosh before losing patience and threatening to flay the boy alive. Instantly the Latinate is dropped for an earthy vernacular: 'Whoa, there, Maister! Aw! Zaint Marsault zuccour me! Ho, ho. In Gawd's name. Lemme be! Don'ee touch me!'[19]

After a less than encouraging visit to an astrologer, Panurge begs Frère Jean, 'in a tremulous voice while scratching his left ear, "Perk me up a while, you old fat-guts. I feel all mentally mataeobefuddledized ..."'[20] Rabelais's characters talk like this all the time, deftly interweaving vulgarity with high erudition. 'Mataeobefuddledized' is an invention, of course. Yet, even if unaware that the prefix 'mataeo' signifies 'vain or unprofitable', we understand exactly how Panurge is feeling. Somehow, 'befuddled' just isn't enough. Rabelais takes words in French, Latin or some other language, or even in combinations of a couple of languages at once, and turbo-charges them, investing them with greater emotional power, sometimes almost to breaking point. He is always enlarging, expanding, complicating, as if ordinary language isn't up to the task of expressing his exuberance and love of life.

But then, Rabelais lived at a time of extraordinary linguistic inventiveness. During the sixteenth and seventeenth centuries, vernacular speech and the secret argots of the criminal underworld were being recorded and studied by scholars for the first time. The interest in foreign tongues that accompanied the huge expansion of trade may well have had a strong element of cultural imperialism, as John Taylor complained, but it was also driven by genuine curiosity.

Shakespeare, Rabelais's heir, is credited with inventing 1700 new words, although how such a figure was arrived at is anyone's guess. We hardly notice them these days, partly because so many have been incorporated into everyday speech and partly because he slots them into complex, poetic sentences in such a way that we glide over them without a thought. All the same, we can't take that figure at face value. In many cases, he was just the first to write down words that were already doing the rounds – it's the speech of the streets that is the crucible of linguistic invention. Sometimes he turned existing nouns into verbs (which is still going on, much to the annoyance of pedants – 'referencing' is a recent example), or verbs into adjectives, or he simply combined existing words to form compounds, such as foulmouthed, leapfrog, time-honoured and barefaced. Among his nonsense words, hodge-podge, hurly burly and boggler have survived, while miching, mallecho, noddles, wittolly and skimble skamble have, unfortunately, fallen by the wayside. 'Skimble skamble', which appears in *King Henry IV, part 1*, illustrates a technique Shakespeare almost certainly picked up from Rabelais. Skamble was an old word meaning confused and rambling, to which Shakespeare added the invented skimble just to make it ramble a bit more, while adding nothing to the meaning. Later writers, on the same principle, gave us pitter-patter, tittle-tattle, wishy-washy, teeny-weeny, super-duper, namby-pamby, hoity-toity, and countless others.

In *Love's Labour's Lost*, an absurdly pretentious conversation between the schoolteacher Holofernes and his friend Sir Nathaniel is mocked by Costard, a simple country lad with a suspiciously broad vocabulary: 'O, they have lived long on the alms-basket of words. I marvel thy master hath not eaten thee for a word; for thou art not so long by the head as honorificabilitudinitatibus: thou art easier swallowed than a flap-dragon.' Not many theatregoers, then or now, could be expected to know what honorificabilitudinitatibus means and Shakespeare must surely have popped it in for a lark. It's from a medieval Latin word meaning 'capable of achieving honours'. Strictly speaking, it's not a nonsense word, but it is doing a good impression of one. Flap-dragon, by the way, was a game involving eating hot raisins from a bowl of burning brandy. They played hard in Shakespeare's day.

There are several 'random Shakespearean insult generators' on the internet, which combine his words into pithy phrases that you can use to express your contempt, provided you don't mind coming across as a pompous prat. One Reginald Unterseher has thoughtfully set sixty-two of them to music and posted them on YouTube. The Bard was clearly not someone you wanted to get on the wrong side of: not unless you wanted to be branded a churlish, clay-brained clotpole; a froward, frothy flapmouth; a pockmarked, puking footlicker; a mewling, motley measlemonger; a bawdy scut; a paunchy pignut; a spongy, spur-galled skainsmate; a hedge-born harpy; or an ill-nurtured, goatish, gleeking, haggard, milk-livered, surly, spleeny, fly-bitten, rank, reeky, gorbellied lout.[21] The barbs of modern politicians are drearily uninventive by comparison.

It was Shakespeare who gave most of these words their first outing in print, including mealy-mouthed and the now common puking.

Using invented words is a great way to show off. Shakespeare was no doubt very pleased with his language skills and had the theatre in which to broadcast them. You can almost hear him preening. But made-up words can also conceal, by excluding all but the initiated. At the very least they can give the impression of intimacy. Jonathan Swift's letters to his mistress Esther Johnson, whom he called 'Stella', use a kind of pidgin of his own devising: 'and zoo must cly Lele and Hele aden. Must loo mimitate pdfr, pay? (and you must cry There and Here again. Must you imitate Presto [Swift], pray?).' The translation doesn't make much more sense than the original, really, but presumably Stella got something out of it or she wouldn't have put up with it for as long as she did. Like a lot of these so-called invented languages, it's not all that difficult to work out once you get the hang of it. That didn't matter to Swift. His aim was simply to take Stella into his confidence, to show her that they had something that nobody else could share. Perhaps it is playful rather than silly.

My parents used to jokingly refer to an umbrella as an umbershoot. That it came from *Ulysses* would have meant nothing to them. How is it that a word can migrate from a banned avant-garde novel to a philistine lower middle-class Melbourne household in just a couple of decades? The process by which certain nonsense words become naturalised while others, no less promising, disappear is completely mysterious. My parents didn't take up 'whenceness', Joyce's word for the place one comes from, nor 'yogibogeybox', the kit of a Freemason (although I don't suppose they would have had much use for that one). Being primly teetotal, they would not have approved of 'peloothered', Joyce's rollicking term for being very drunk.

While I can understand why 'abnihilisation' and 'engauzements' (as in 'she cancelled all her engauzements') never caught on, I would have thought 'joyicity', 'alcoherent', 'clownsillies' and 'pringlepik' were contenders. 'Quark', a nonsense word from *Finnegans Wake* ('Three quarks for Muster Mark!') has been co-opted by astro-physicists, and 'Mr Right' seized on by dating agencies (although I wonder if that one was really Joyce's invention).

Joyce plays with words in Latin, Danish, French, German, Italian, Gaelic, Finnish, Hebrew and one or two more obscure languages. Not that he was familiar with them all, he just picked up bits and pieces from books and friends, anything that took his fancy. William Tindall calls *Finnegans Wake* 'a music of words in which ideas play second fiddle', and that music cannot be properly appreciated by picking out funny words in isolation, as I've been doing. One punning word plays off another, each inflecting and distorting the meanings of its companions to create a symphonic structure of dizzying complexity, as this virtually incomprehensible explanation from Tindall's guide confirms:

> The matter of the first paragraph on p. 4 is heroic conflict, whether of siege, 'camibalistics' or boomerangs, followed by peace, as rise follows fall. The conflicts include Ostrogoths against Visigoths; oysters against fish and frogs (there by the croaking chorus of Aristophanes); Irishmen (White Boys of Howth and 'Sod's brood'. 'Fear' is

Gaelic Fir, men); Protestant against Catholic (*Ego te absolvo* indicates the Catholics while 'Bid me to love', a distortion of a song by Herrick, means Protestant ...); Jacob against Esau again (hair and 'false jiccup') ... But the sky-signs of Times Square or Piccadilly promise peace and renewal as does Isabel (Tristan's 'Iseut') and her soeurs ('sewers'). 'Phall if you will, but rise you must' ... suggests free will, necessity, and the phallus, echoed by 'pharce', the farce of destiny and the Pharos of Alexandria. 'Phoenish', the key word, combines finish and phoenix.[22]

And that's just the first paragraph of page 4. We have another 624 pages to go.

Trifling with the vocabulary

The passage above confirms Joyce as an inveterate punster: '... when they were yung and easily freudened', from *Finnegans Wake*, is one of my favourites of his.

Punsters always seem to be inveterate, don't they, when they are not being compulsive, obsessive or habitual. There is an ingrained cultural prejudice against this particular form of wordplay that insists on turning it into a pathology. For every pun there must be a punishment. Perhaps it's because most of the puns we are subjected to – and we are subjected to an awful lot – are so teeth-grindingly bad, and we are apt to be unappreciative of what can be good about bad puns.

A pun is simply a playful confusion of two or more words that sound similar but have different meanings, such as when 'Pulitzer Prize' becomes 'Pullet Surprise' (a justly famous one, that, because it so wickedly takes the mickey out of something normally accorded solemn respect), or when a child names her cross-eyed bear Gladly after the old hymn, 'Gladly my Cross I'd bear'. Some of the cleverest puns use words that sound identical (homonyms) in different contexts, such as Groucho Marx's, 'Time flies like an arrow, fruit flies like a banana'.

Like most wordplay, puns are frivolous. They serve no purpose other than to make people laugh, or groan, and, of course, to show off the cleverness and disruptiveness of the perpetrator. They are a stick poked annoyingly into the smooth-turning cogs of a conversation. 'Puns are threatening because puns reveal the arbitrariness of meaning', writes John Pollack, author of *The Pun also Rises*, 'and the layers of nuance that can be packed onto a single word. So people who dislike puns tend to be people who seek a level of control that doesn't exist. If you have an approach to the world that is rules-based, driven by hierarchy and threatened by irreverence, then you're not going to like puns.' Or any other kind of silliness, for that matter.

It has to be said, however, that puns can also be used to express impatience or hide ignorance. If the conversation appears to be getting a bit too serious or erudite, a well-placed pun will effectively bring it back to earth. Puns can be a way of asserting control.

They are surely one of the oldest forms of wordplay. They were part of the rhetorical armoury of the ancient Greeks and Romans. Cicero used puns to great effect, although those of his that have survived sound pretty lame to modern ears. You probably had to be there. Like Plautus a century or so earlier, and Aristophanes a couple of centuries before that, Cicero seemed to delight in self-consciously bad puns for the pleasure of trying his audience's patience (a somewhat risky strategy, it would seem, for a political orator). When Aristophanes, in *The Wasps*, has Bdelycleon advising his jurist father (in the English translation) that, 'if it's a fine sunny morning you can dispense some summery justice', you can almost hear the collective groan rising from the tiers. The self-consciously bad pun is a way of saying, yes, I know it's atrocious but we're all in this together. What makes it funny is our mutual acknowledgement that it is not funny at all, but that we intend to carry on as if it is. We are laughing at our own complicity.

Naturally, puns were a favourite with jesters and fools in the Middle Ages, being a great way to insult and defame people while still being able to claim, if challenged, that your intentions were entirely innocent. There is safety in being able to hide behind ambiguity.

Only when printing created the need to standardise the English language did ambiguity start to become a problem. 'To trifle with the vocabulary which is the vehicle of social intercourse is to tamper with the currency of human intelligence,' Dr Johnson declaimed, which is not only pompous but dead wrong. Aristophanes, that manic trifler, would certainly not have agreed with him, nor would Shakespeare. As compiler of the *Dictionary of the English Language*, Johnson was keen to impose order, which in 1755 was sorely needed. But that's no reason his view should still hold sway today.

Johnson may have been taking a pot shot at his older contemporary Jonathan Swift, whom he disliked intensely. It's not hard to see why: Swift was a great one for trifling with the vocabulary, and adored puns. His 'Modest Defence of Punning', published in 1716, was intended as a gleeful two-finger salute to the literati of the day, who considered wordplay of this kind beneath contempt. 'Modest Defence', written in response to a fellow member of parliament's attack on punning, is in itself a catalogue of outrageous puns (which Swift helpfully, if didactically, italicises). Many will go over the heads of modern readers, who cannot be expected to know, for example, that a besom is a type of broom.

> But I think I may let pass his *Petty* Accounts of the great Plague, where five Millions as he says were *Swept* away, which indeed Mr. Alexander *Broom* records, thô there *be some* who deny it, and think it a *Whisker* yet every body allow it to have been a terrible *Brush*, and that it made clean work, especially in *Birchin* Lane.[23]

Swift regularly held punning contests with his godson, Thomas Sheridan, who thought that everyone should be made to come up with six puns every evening before being allowed to sit down to dinner. Elder sons who could not do so, he declared, should be disinherited and the estate given to the next hopeful child.

Unless you are aware of Swift's fondness for puns, sexually suggestive ones in particular, the repeated references to Master Bates at the beginning of *Gulliver's Travels* will seem perfectly innocent. It is this very pretence of innocence that gives puns their bite, and makes the sexually suggestive pun the most effective kind. If we choose to misinterpret, that's our fault. Clearly we're the ones with dirty minds.

'Fuckin' hell' is not something you'd expect to hear on prime-time television, for instance, certainly not in 1975 anyway. But when the Two Ronnies, after a careful set-up, sang, 'The swans were swimming on the far canal – far canal!' (it was an old line even then), there could be no legitimate complaint. What? We had no idea! Although they knew that we knew that they knew.

A blonde bimbo sitting up in bed next to a startled-looking Benny Hill asks, 'What is *this* thing called, love?' The director shouts, 'Cut! No, no, no, it's "What *is* this thing called love?"' The British are masters of this kind of unsubtle but devilishly clever innuendo: more than a century of sexual repression having got them well primed. Perhaps, though, the moment has passed. These days we are less tolerant of suggestiveness. Fuckin' hell is fuckin' hell, and something has been lost as a result.

Newspaper headlines and the names of restaurants and hair salons are fertile breeding grounds for everyday punsters. Why cafe owners and hairdressers should be particularly susceptible I have no idea, except that the words 'Thai' and 'hair' offer such a wealth of irresistible temptations. There must be thousands of Thai-Tanics, Thaiphoons and Bar Celona's out there. Tequila Mockingbird (in the USA) is perfect for a Mexican-themed bar, Basic Kneads is good for a baker, but Lard Have Mercy (for a spare-ribs cafe) sounds as if it was dreamt up late one night after a lot of booze and somehow failed to get discarded in the morning. Recently I spotted 'Poultry in Motion' on a van delivering frozen chickens to the local supermarket. I would certainly patronise a fish and chip shop called Frying Nemo (were it not in England), although that perhaps isn't, strictly speaking, a pun. On the other hand, Lord of the Fries, at Melbourne Central, is perhaps not such a wise choice, especially as it advertises itself as 'good for kids'.

The most famous, and most copied, salon name is Curl up and Dye, which made its first brief appearance in the *Blues Brothers* movie in 1980 and has never looked back. But doesn't it suggest curling up and dying with embarrassment when you look in the mirror and see what they've done to you? Hair Apparent, Go Ahead and Urban Roots are more positive, but Hair Today suggests, by implication, that the place might not be there the next time you need a trim.

Some funny combinations are purely fortuitous, such as Hart and Haley, one-time Western Sydney real estate agents, and A.E. Grocock and Son, Artificial Limb Makers (I'm not making this up), who were listed in the Sydney telephone directory in the 1970s. They could hardly have been unaware.

Whether clever or excruciating, punning business names are wonderfully cheering. They radiate camaraderie. 'We don't take ourselves too seriously,' they say, 'and we know you're smart, and forgiving, enough to appreciate the joke: you're one of us.'

Although Rupert Murdoch is not renowned for his empathy or wit, we have him to thank, or blame, for the explosion of punning newspaper headlines over the past two or three decades. It seems sub-editors just can't help themselves. As you might expect, the vast majority are cruel and unfunny (one or the other might be forgivable but not both). 'Elton takes David up the Aisle', for a piece on Elton John's wedding, has just the right degree of vulgarity, but for puns of real wit and warmth we have to look beyond the tabloids.

I have vague memories of a snippet in *Rolling Stone* sometime during the 1970s about Gloria Steinem throwing up over an airline steward, headed 'Sick transit Gloria'. In those days even a rock-music magazine could assume some religious sophistication among its readership. *The Times Literary Supplement*, in a flash of genius, headed a review of a book about George Bernard Shaw's private life with, 'The Wilder Loves of Shaw'. One of my favourite headlines, because it does achieve a childlike charm, is from the *Los Angeles Times*: 'Big Rig carrying Fruit crashes on 210 Freeway, creates Jam'.

Glorumptious

When you bump two words together, sparks fly. Does Joyce's 'phoenish' signify an ending or a beginning, both at once, or an ending leading to a new beginning? At this level of inventiveness, portmanteau words are, like puns, to which they are closely related, a playful up-yours to signification, throwing us into confusion, making a mockery of our certitude. Phoenish would have met with the approval of Humpty Dumpty. 'You see,' he explains, in *Alice Through the Looking Glass*, 'it's like a portmanteau – there are two meanings packed up into one word.' Loath as I am to quibble with Mr Dumpty, who after all was the one who first drew the analogy, it isn't always so. Sometimes, the word formed suggests much the same as its component words, and putting them together gives them extra punch, as in Dahl's glorumptious. It's the comedy of excess.

Comic portmanteau words happily draw attention to their own cleverness: they are look-at-me words. You can't just read past them and ignore them, you have to stop, if only for an instant, to work them out. And the reward, if you're lucky, will be a guffaw or a wry smile.

Sadly, most of them these days are not comic but leaden. Marketers and IT nerds, in their rush for compression, are depressingly fond of collapsing two words into one, saddling us with biopic, Brexit, infomercial, jazzercise, alcopop and all the rest: clunky non-words that quickly enter the language and just as quickly disappear when they've had their day.

Beth Tovey, from the Oxford Dictionary, points out that

real nonsense words rarely enter the language, which is why Edward Lear, for example, contributed hardly any new words to the OED. Perhaps he is not the best example because, like Lewis Carroll (*Jabberwocky* notwithstanding), Lear preferred to use existing words in absurd contexts rather than inventing new ones. Yet that needn't detract from her general contention that, 'nonsense words are, by their nature, not the kind of thing that a dictionary deals with. They are often indefinable, used by an individual writer as part of his or her linguistic repertoire, and don't necessarily gain any wider currency.'[24] Well, not immediately anyway. As Shakespeare proved, nonsense words do sometimes become normalised over time.

All the same, we are unlikely any time soon to be bandying about in conversation Rabelais's 'circumbilivaginating' (meaning, ironically enough, high-flown speech) or his suggestive 'foolosophers', Joyce's 'alcoherent', Roald Dahl's 'delumptious', or Homer Simpson's wickedly clever 'sacrilicious'.

Silliness mans up

Lewis Carroll's *Jabberwocky* is crammed full of nonsense words that come tumbling after one another in a rush, like a horde of those apocryphal lemmings hurling themselves over a cliff. Besides 'brillig', there's 'mimsy', 'outgrabe', 'frumious', 'uffish', 'galumphing' and 'tumtum' tree, just for starters. Of a total of twenty-three words in the first verse, only five (if we discount 'and' and 'the') are standard English. Yet the whole thing manages to hang together, not making sense, exactly, but painting a vivid picture. And the picture it paints is of a misty medieval world of knights and dragons, especially in later verses, when, 'The Jabberwock, with eyes of flame,/ came whiffling through the tulgy wood,/ And burbled as it came.' Carroll had an interest in medieval literature and the original version of *Jabberwocky*, published long before he adapted it for *Alice Through the Looking Glass*, imitates the sounds and spellings of early, German-inflected English. He could rely on the sympathetic interest of his young readers at a time when the Gothic Revival and the Pre-Raphaelites had made the Middle Ages sexy. Not even nonsense is immune to fashion.

Now, compare the connotative overload of *Jabberwocky* with the more tangible images conjured up in Edward Lear's *The Owl and the Pussycat*, of which this is the final verse:

> 'Dear Pig, are you willing to sell for one shilling
>   Your ring?' Said the Piggy, 'I will.'
> So they took it away, and were married next day
>   By the Turkey who lives on the hill.
> They dined on mince, and slices of quince,
>   Which they ate with a runcible spoon;
> And hand in hand, on the edge of the sand,
>   They danced by the light of the moon,
>   The moon,
>   They danced by the light of the moon.

This is all delightfully silly. Yet, setting aside the reference to a Bong tree in verse two, runcible is the only invented word in the entire poem. It pops up unexpectedly like an exploding sherbet bomb, all the more effective for its isolation. Runcible is one nonsense word of Lear's that has made it into the dictionary, although T.S. Eliot later borrowed it to describe his hat and it's as good for a hat as it is for a spoon.

Lear's and Carroll's delightful worlds of fantasy could

very easily be construed as reactionary, designed to deflect delicate young minds from the horrors of factory labour and the workhouse. The otherworldliness of silliness always leaves it open to the charge of escapism. But it's too simple to accuse Carroll and Lear of complacency. Rather they conjure an alternative world, where the kind of brutal logic that determines political action has no purchase. The invention of words capable of meaning whatever anyone might choose them to mean makes the point explicit. This is, in effect, a form of passive resistance.

And yet, and yet! Alice, Humpty Dumpty and the Poggle who has no toes belong irretrievably to the nineteenth century, don't they. Their sweetness and whimsy are no match for world wars, the Great Depression and the Gulag. Even silliness had to man up a bit for the terrible twentieth century. If Victorian literary silliness was mainly directed at children, its Modernist counterpart was a much more grown-up affair.

Just eighty years after the Owl and the Pussycat sailed away in their beautiful pea-green boat, Neddy Seagoon, Major Bloodnok, Eccles and Bluebottle were doing battle with the Dreaded Batter-Pudding Hurler. A lot had happened in the intervening eighty years, and the Goons inhabited a darker, more disillusioned world. Their nihilistic, who-gives-a-toss clowning, while it poses as innocent fun, is laced with a very English anxiety about the Cold War and the atom bomb. Spike Milligan, the Goons' mentor and principal writer, favours nonsense words that are defiantly *un*inventive, the kind of simple, rhythmic sound clusters that spring readily to the minds of children. Therein lies their charm, and their hidden sting.

SILLINESS: A SERIOUS HISTORY

Take, for example, the *Ying Tong Song*, originally performed on *The Goon Show*, then subsequently taking on a life of its own, reaching number 3 on the UK singles chart in 1956. The chorus, endlessly repeated, goes like this:

> *Ying tong ying tong*
> *Ying tong ying tong*
> *Ying tong iddle I po,*
> *Ying tong ying tong*
> *Ying tong ying tong*
> *Ying tong iddle I po*

What makes it funny is its crushing banality, as if Milligan couldn't even be bothered making up interesting nonsense words. While there are echoes of Lear's childishness (his Bong Tree, for example), there is also a very adult knowingness (along with some subtle mockery of the Chinese language, mirroring the Indian-mockery in Lear).

As if embarrassed by its own vacuity, the *Ying Tong Song* tarts itself up with the most extraordinary panoply of bells and whistles: a lush orchestral introduction, trumpet fanfares, drum rolls, a flurry of energetic bluegrass, an operatic interlude, farts (of course – it is English, after all), cannon fire, the clatter of running feet and a loud explosion to bring it all to a rousing conclusion. All of which manages only to emphasise its inconsequentiality.

The great attraction of a poem like Milligan's *On the Ning Nang Nong* is that you could just as easily have come up with it yourself while sitting on the loo before breakfast. It begins:

Too Silly for Words

On the Ning Nang Nong
Where the Cows go Bong!
And the Monkeys all say Boo!
There's a Nong Nang Ning
Where the trees go Ping!
And the tea pots Jibber Jabber Joo.[25]

It's no wonder a nationwide poll in 1998 voted this the UK's favourite comic poem, ahead of anything by Lear or Carroll. While we are quite prepared to be humbled by the cleverness of an Agatha Christie mystery or the psychological complexity of *King Lear*, we like silliness to do pretty much what we can do. We like to identify with the writer of silliness. However wildly inventive and incomprehensible he or she may be, we never feel excluded. It's all a game, a game without rules, in which we feel welcome to participate in whatever way we choose. So our 'I-could-do-that' response is not tinged with resentment, as it might be before certain works of contemporary art, because we do not feel that someone is trying to bully us. We are simply being invited to join the fun.

If Spike Milligan conceals his disenchantment beneath a colourful cloak of childishness, Roald Dahl frankly acknowledges – in fact revels in – the inherent cruelty of the young. Like Milligan, Dahl was scarred by wartime experiences, but for him childhood, far from being a welcome retreat from adult vileness, is its wellspring.

Few authors can boast a dictionary devoted to their oeuvre. *The Oxford Roald Dahl Dictionary* lists hundreds of made-up words, along with many standard English ones that Dahl presses into novel uses. What's striking is how many are designed to scare the pants off his young readers. No rose-coloured spectacles for him. Bloodbottlers and Fleshlumpeaters, for example, are bogrotting (very unpleasant) monsters of the kind you might come across if you're having a bogthumper (a horrid nightmare) or a trogglehumper (an even worse nightmare, possibly involving children being eaten alive). It's all so horrigust it's enough to get any human bean flussed.

Even rare and harmless creatures such as the polly-frog, the bobolink, the skrock, and the (less friendly but equally endangered) venomous squerkle are at risk of having their body parts harvested by Willy Wonka to make Vita-Wonk, an oily medicine that causes premature ageing, or Wonka-Vite, which, of course, has the opposite effect. A key ingredient of Wonka-Vite is sprunge, secreted by young slimescrapers.

As every child knows, however, unpleasantness can always be turned to advantage. How many youngsters, to the dismay of their parents, have adopted trogfilth, pigsquibble and swatchwallop to protest at the filthsome food they are being made to eat? 'By goggles,' cries the BFG – or Big Friendly Giant – when he first savours the delunctiousness of sausages and eggs, 'this stuff is making snozzcumbers [cucumber-like vegetables that have been his only sustenance until now] taste like swatchwallop!'

The energy and inventiveness is positively Rabelaisian. Dahl employs every trick there is: as well as puns and portmanteau words, there are malapropisms (langwitch), spoonerisms (piggery-jokery and Dahl's chickens, the English author) and onomatopoeic words (glissing, from the French *glisser*, to slide, for gliding slimily). He resurrects obsolete words in English (swudge, for example, is a sweet paste used to make edible lawn: a blend of the old word sward with fudge). He spells words backwards (Esio Trot). He adds bogus suffixes and prefixes (sickable and umpossible) and he happily jumbles compound nouns (ringbeller and curdbloodling). Finally, he picks up obscure words he finds suggestive and lends them new meanings, such as grunion, which is a type of fish in the real world but a grumpy individual in Dahl's.

Something he rarely does, however, is to borrow directly from foreign languages, as Rabelais and Joyce did all the time. Dahl is very Anglo-centric. Perhaps he felt that English had absorbed enough foreign words already. Dahl's aim is to provide children with a secret language of their own that excludes adults, while encouraging them to expand on it with words and phrases of their own. Perhaps he sticks to English as his jumping-off point because he doesn't want to make things too complicated.

Happy disrupters

So, take your pick: is it to be a portmanteau word that packs two words together; or a pun that draws two meanings out of one word; or gibberish, that has – or at least aspires to – no meaning at all? Or would you prefer something onomatopoeic that sounds like what it describes; as when a prostitute in *Ulysses* is found, 'whispering lovewords murmur liplapping loudly, poppysmic plopslop'? There are dozens of ways to make up new words and although they are, in the end, all crafted from the same twenty-four letters of the alphabet, the possibilities are unlimited.

The one thing most of them have in common is their musicality. They are for saying – or singing or shouting or declaiming – more than for reading. Swift told his mistress that when he wrote to her in their invented language he always formed his mouth into the shape of the words as he put them down, revelling in their sounds, as if he were speaking to her. It turned their correspondence into conversation. Regular words, bandied about in books, pamphlets, petitions and public notices, simply wouldn't have provided the same degree of intimacy. Meaning wasn't the most important consideration, it was sensibility he wanted to convey.

In this sense, then, nonsense words are a protest against the standardising effects of print (to which Swift had a lifelong aversion, despite his many printed works). They are a principled disordering, or a subversive extension, of the dictionary. While they existed before printing, of course, as children's rhymes amply demonstrate, print culture gave nonsense words their role as happy disrupters of the most complex and rule-bound of human systems. Which is why their first great flourishing was in the early eighteenth century when print was first coming into general use.

Be assured, nonsense words, although lots of fun, are more than just bugswallop.

Four   **ONLY DISCONNECT**

> So she went into the garden to cut a cabbage leaf, to make an apple pie; and at the same time a great she-bear coming up the street, pops its head into the shop. 'What! no soap?' So he died, and she very imprudently married the barber; and there were present the Picninnies, and the Joblillies, and the Garyulies, and the grand Panjandrum himself, with the little round button at top; and they all fell to playing the game of catch as catch can, till the gunpowder ran out at the heels of their boots.

Pure delightful silliness, to be sure. Yet its author, the early-eighteenth-century dramatist and theatre manager Samuel Foote, did in fact have a purpose in mind: he was trying to trip up an actor who had boasted that he could remember any text after a single reading. Whether Foote succeeded I don't know, but he did manage to pen a minor classic of silliness.

Although Foote throws in a couple of made-up words – 'Panjandrum', a word he invented, has since made it into the dictionary – they are not what makes it funny. (For what it's worth, I find 'imprudently' the most amusing word here.) It's not really about words. What we have, instead, is a string of phrases that, although coherent in themselves, have been put together with no regard to how they connect, so that one thing fails to follow logically from another. *Non sequiturs* are almost always funny because they expose the fragility of our reason.

Although it fails to add up, Foote's fractured story does create a montage of pictures in our minds. Because it maintains a tenuous hold on reality we persist in trying to assemble its various incidents into some kind of whole, aware all the while that this just isn't going to happen. It shows all the signs of having originated as a game of consequences, where each player contributes a line without knowing what's been written on the line above, so that, despite a certain grammatical continuity, the narrative quickly disintegrates.

All the same, it is different from the silliness of Lewis Carroll and Edward Lear, by which I mean different *in kind*. Carroll's and Lear's flights of fancy, although decidedly odd, still manage to hang together. However wacky the events in Wonderland, the prose that describes them is lucid and the narrative coherent. Foote's fragmentary tale, on the other hand, is closer to the Modernist approach of Beckett and Joyce, which consciously draws attention to the mechanics of the language by taking it apart to examine its wheels and cogs, leaving us with an apparently random assemblage of narrative bits and pieces to sort out for ourselves. Lear's and Carroll's approach exploits language's poetic potential, while Beckett's and Joyce's tries to expose language's limitations. While the first takes us on a luxury cruise to exotic places, the second makes us work for our passage on a vessel whose destination is not immediately apparent.

Firstly, then, let's take the luxury cruise.

The mask of silliness

Who hasn't experienced that moment of moral panic when the life of the party, who has been entertaining everyone all evening with pranks and witticisms, is suddenly revealed as seriously disturbed? Without warning, the bonhomie turns creepy. Silliness can sometimes be a cover for actual mental distress.

I always feel uneasy watching Spike Milligan being interviewed for television in his whiskery later years. On a live chat show in 1989 he runs rings around a young Joanna Lumley, scoring laughs at her expense and leaving her looking awkward and inept. When a polite but insistent young man gatecrashes the set to promote a children's charity, Spike at first appears sympathetic. 'Come and see me after the show,' he calls, as the boy is led away, adding, *sotto voce*, 'and I'll beat the shit out of you.' The audience response is a little nervous. They want it to be a joke, as Spike insists it is, but it's not funny and the undercurrent of bitterness is all too apparent.

Bitterness and depression are undisguised in Peter Cook's laconic ramblings on the radio about fish. Towards the end of his career, when most of his time was spent drinking alone while watching television, Cook regularly, and anonymously, rang a late-night talkback show pretending to be a Norwegian insomniac named Sven. He was pleased to be in England, he said, where he could escape the fish that infested every aspect of life back home. Talkback programs there were entirely devoted to fish – is a carp very big, or is a tench very big, or how big is a guppy? Not to mention a one-hour children's program every afternoon about gefilte fish. Even football matches are interrupted by lectures about fish. One positive outcome is that hooliganism is unknown in Norway because all the fish programs are so boring they calm people down. Sven's other ongoing complaint is about his wife, Jutta, who has left him: 'for some fish'. Sven is travelling the world in a futile search for Jutta. 'Do you deal with fish problems?' he asks, in his lugubrious Scandinavian drawl.

Sven's maudlin humour can come across as uncomfortably close to the bone now we know who he is, although some listeners must have suspected something fishy was going on (the program's presenter eventually discovered Sven's true identity, but kept the secret). Peter Cook is a professional comedian: one of the best. But he gets no money or recognition from his Sven character, he is not aware that the calls are being recorded, and his listeners don't know it's meant to be a joke. So who is it all for? Cook is talking to himself, trying to resolve his personal problems through the intervention of a fictional character.

So long as we are confident that the speaker or writer is a sane, well-balanced person, we can safely interpret silliness as humour and laugh along. But if we suspect they are motivated by desperation, or are mentally ill, we know better than to laugh. In short, we may laugh *with*, but not *at*. It's a distinction we have to master if we're going to get on in the world without injury.

Part of the job of the comic writer or performer is to bridge the gap. Are Pantagruel and Panurge mad? What about Don Quixote? Quite possibly. They certainly behave as if they are. Yet we are free to laugh at their antics because we know they are the creations of authors who have a wider purpose in mind. The intercession of an author grants us leave to laugh at the mad, the senile and the immature without any uncomfortable feelings of guilt. An intelligent, rational person is presenting us with a simulacrum – madness at one remove – like the fool at a medieval court.

There are, I am reliably informed, nearly thirty plays in English from the seventeenth century that include the rantings of mad people. Most are intended as comic relief, and audiences at the time would no doubt have found them amusing while pondering their oddly melancholic poetry.

For example, Castruccio and Fluello, a couple of aristocratic toffs in the early seventeenth-century play *The Honest Whore*, finding themselves at a loose end, pay a visit to Bethlem. There, three madmen entertain them with lengthy dissertations on porridge, parrots, and fingernails:

> Such nails had my middlemost son and I made him a promoter, and he scrap'd, and scrap'd, and scrap'd till he got the devil and all, but he scrap'd thus, and thus, and thus, and it went under his legs, till at length a company of kites taking him for carrion swept up all, all, all, all, all, all.

For educated folk, attuned to the contemporary academic interest in language, the madman's rant would have been more than just a voyeuristic entertainment. The fact that it was part of a play, written by a rational playwright for a rational actor who is pretending to be irrational, gave them a degree of licence.

So, while silliness as we understand it today is not the same as madness, there is a sometimes discomforting connection, and it's not too much of a stretch to say that silliness springs, in part, from early *representations* of madness.

Getting the right balance

Silliness was not entirely the prerogative of the well educated, as nursery rhymes and popular songs attest. Admittedly, many of them made more sense two or three hundred years ago than they do now. Meanings drain away as the years pass. Yesterday's common sense might well be today's absurdity.

Yet, the urge to rationalise appears to have got completely out of hand. For every rhyme and ditty there is now a welter of explanations of what it 'actually' means, a lot of them gruesome and a good many of them baseless. Hundreds of books and websites are dedicated to squeezing the last drops of cultural significance from the apparent nonsense of the early modern period: *The Secret Life of Mother Goose*, *The Dark Origins of Classic Nursery Rhymes*, *Meanings and History Behind Children's Rhymes* and so on. That people might have just been having a bit of fun is apparently not an option, despite the fact that we know the eighteenth century, in particular, to have been more responsive to the irrational than we are today. It's like explaining the 'real' meaning of Monty Python's Fish-Slapping Dance – useful up to a point, I suppose, and potentially quite enlightening, but a bit beside the point unless you're a cultural studies student, for whom nothing can be allowed to speak for itself. The modern obsession with finding a rational explanation for everything becomes slightly tedious after a while and a lot of good nonsense is ruined by exegesis. Sometimes a jape is just a jape.

So let us simply rejoice in the sheer magic of the two horses making lace in the old nursery rhyme, the house that bows to a squire and the little boy who puts his finger in his eye and pulls out golden fishes (actually a toned-down version of an earlier ditty in which a young maid puts her finger in a different orifice altogether). And, while we are enjoying such frolics, the scholars and historians can safely be left to puzzle over their hidden significance.

With comic literature, we are on firmer ground, for we know who the authors were and we can have some idea of their intentions. For example, there can be little doubt that Rabelais is just horsing around when he has Pantagruel's young chum Panurge hold his glasses to his left ear so he can hear more clearly. Or when the postmaster, in Gogol's *Dead Souls*, almost succeeds in convincing the town's worthies that the mysterious visitor Chichikov is actually the fully limbed Captain Kopeikin, despite it having already been established that Kopeikin had an arm and leg blown off in the 1812 campaign. Or when Pat, in *Alice in Wonderland*, calls out that he is in the garden digging for apples. Or when Sergeant Pluck, in Flann O'Brien's *The Third Policeman*, expounds the five rules of wisdom: 'Always ask any questions that are to be asked and never answer any. Turn everything you hear to your own advantage. Always carry a repair outfit. Take left turns as much as possible. Never apply your front brake first.'[26]

Surely it can't be too difficult to come up with funny anecdotes like this. *Non sequiturs* are easy. You don't have to have a mind as sharp as Lewis Carroll's. All you have to do is establish a situation, then fracture as many logical connections as you can. Or so it would seem. But it is not just a matter of letting loose with whatever craziness comes to mind. Some discipline is necessary. We don't want to get lost in meaninglessness altogether. Silliness, if it's to be funny, involves playing with the rules of logic and representation in a way that suggests a range of possible meanings while ultimately exposing all of them as untenable. The more tension there is between the promise of logical exposition and the frustration of our expectations the more amused we are likely to be.

This is why dreams fail to qualify. When a friend tells us he dreamt of being chased by a randy donkey, found himself rooted to the spot when he tried to flee and was carried off in the nick of time by a giant bird, we just wonder idly whether he's been eating too much spicy food, or not getting his leg over as much he'd like. After all, this is just the way dreams are – fluid and uncontrollable – so the tension is lacking. However, the same scenario in a *Looney Tunes* cartoon, contextualised in a broader narrative, might very well be funny.

Sir Arthur Streeb-Greebling (aka Peter Cook) gets the balance right in an interview he did with a somewhat bemused Ludovic Kennedy for BBC2 in 1990. There's just enough grounding in reality to make the absurdity work. Sir Arthur blithely recalls his negligent father, who insisted on him being raised by wolves. 'Fortunately for me,' he says, 'there were very few decent-sized wolves in the Aylesbury area at the time. In fact, the only thing that even remotely resembled a wolf was my Aunt Mary's Pekinese and my father, in his wisdom, drew the line at me being suckled by a Pekinese.'

> *Really? Why?*
> I don't know. I don't think it was a racial thing. He had great respect for the Pekinese. They were the Chinese hunting dogs, you know.
> *Were they?*
> Oh yes. Bred to track down the hippopotami that infested the Fuzhou valley and drag them out of their warrens.

Hence the huge, boggling eyes they developed.
Yes.

Now a lot of people think the Pekinese developed their huge, boggling eyes in order for them to be able to see in the dark down the hippopotamus warrens, but not so, not so at all. The reason why the Pekinese developed such huge, boggling eyes is purely one of surprise that anyone would ask them to perform such a function. They're terribly small, the Pekinese, and the hippo by contrast is gigantic, and it'd take about five hundred Pekinese working as a team to drag the hippo out of its lair. So my father decided to have me raised by goats.[27]

Peter Cook was at his best when playing an upper-class twit. His partnership with Dudley Moore worked as well as it did because Moore typically played (and indeed was) a working-class lad. It's that old comedic staple, the clash of social registers. Just about every British comedy you can think of depends upon it to one degree or another.

As an Australian, Shaun Micallef does the razor-sharp wordplay without the class obsession. The fact that most of *Mad as Hell*, his weekly program on the ABC, is made up of satirical sketches about current political issues, makes the occasional flights of pure silliness all the more sparky. Micallef is an effortless genre-buster. Amidst swipes at the prime minister and leader of the opposition, you catch something about Entente Cordiale, the blind French plumber who installed the male toilets in the Statue of Liberty's head, and you wonder if that's meant to be a reference to something.

Micallef enjoys playing the pedant, quoting some politician's inane utterance, then, instead of satirising the content, picking apart the grammar to expose the absurdity of statements that would normally glide right by us because we've become so used to being bombarded with meaningless waffle it doesn't even register with us any more. And, if that sentence seems a bit breathless, that's the way Micallef talks. While Peter Cook is the very essence of composure, Micallef is manic. He effortlessly converts stupidity into silliness simply by holding it up to the light so you can see right through it.

Consider this concocted interview with a supposed member of the public after a bomb blast in a suburban street:

> *Ian, tell us what happened.*
> Well, I'd just turned the TV on, I was taking my trousers off, and I heard this almighty explosion. It sounded like a bomb going off.
> *A bomb had gone off.*
> Yeah, I know, I heard it.
> *So it sounded exactly like what it was.*
> Yeah, but I didn't know what had happened.
> *Why wouldn't you have thought a bomb had gone off?*
> Well it sounded like a bomb had gone off, but I didn't know what actually happened.
> *Why couldn't it have been a bomb going off?*
> Well, it only sounded like a bomb going off. It could have been anything.
> *What else could it have been other than a bomb going off? What sounds more like a bomb going off than a bomb going off?*
> I don't know, I've never heard a bomb going off.
> *Yes you have, about an hour ago.*

But before that.

If you've never heard a bomb going off, how did you know it sounded like a bomb going off? You couldn't have, could you.[28]

Looking dazed, the poor sod is dragged away by the police.

Rather than a failure to connect, this is the opposite: a pernickety overload of connections: literal-mindedness taken to extremes. It exposes the everyday slippages in language that make normal conversation possible. If we all behaved like Shaun Micallef, we would hardly be able to communicate with one another at all.

In *The Grim Grotto*, Lemony Snicket's literal-mindedness leads him to a pseudo-scientific explanation of the water cycle that is as circular as what it describes.

> The water cycle consists of three phenomena – evaporation, precipitation, and collection – which are the three phenomena that make up what is known as 'the water cycle'. Evaporation, the first of these phenomena, is the process of water turning into vapor and eventually forming clouds, such as those found in cloudy skies, or on cloudy days, or even cloudy nights. These clouds are formed by a phenomenon known as 'evaporation', which is the first of three phenomena that make up the water cycle. Evaporation, the first of these three, is simply a term for a process by which water turns into vapor and eventually forms clouds. Clouds can be recognized by their appearance, usually on cloudy days or nights, when they can be seen in cloudy skies. The name for the process by which clouds are formed – by water, which turns into vapor and becomes part of the formation known

> as 'clouds' – is 'evaporation', the first phenomenon in the three phenomena that make up the cycle of water, otherwise known as 'the water cycle', ...[29]

The narrator knows full well that the water cycle is a really boring subject. He is explaining it in the hope of sending his young listeners to sleep. It proves effective. But his confident expectation that the reader will also nod off is unlikely to be realised: the reader is in on the joke.

Snicket is Beckett for the post-modern age: Beckett-lite, if you will. He takes the metafictional elements of Modernism and makes them dance a jig. All the familiar ingredients rub shoulders in his books: the mixing of genres that make fiction and non-fiction indistinguishable from one another; the authorial interjections and other kinds of narrative fracturing; the irony that makes it hard to decide what's meant to be taken seriously and what isn't; the self-referentiality; the endless play with language; the black humour and the ghoulish preoccupation with death, violence and misery. The big difference is that, where Beckett's silliness is ultimately depressive, Snicket's is gleeful: even the misery. *The Grim Grotto* begins, 'Dear reader, there is nothing to be found in Lemony Snicket's "A Series of Unfortunate Events" but misery and despair. You still have time to choose another international best-selling series to read.' What child is going to take that on trust?

Never mind the rules

Where would we be without rules? Those of a hippyish bent might lazily insist that rules are there to be broken, yet, without road rules we would be constantly smashing into one another, without rules of proper conduct we would all end up behaving like politicians, and without rules in games and sports, well, there would be no games or sports, which are all rules. As Eugene McCarthy once said about football, you have to be smart enough to know the rules and dumb enough to think they matter.

Lewis Carroll understood that for rules to matter they have to be consistent and everyone involved has to agree to them. Which, of course, is the exact opposite of what applies in Wonderland. There, although the penalties for breaking the rules include instant decapitation, nobody understands them and in any case they keep changing. As a rather prim little girl with a solid Victorian sense of right and wrong, Alice – along with everyone else – should be terrified. On the contrary, she is mostly mildly amused. What's striking is her unflappability when faced with talking caterpillars, lobsters dancing the quadrille, the cat's grin that lingers long after the cat has gone, and her own sudden and vertiginous changes in size. When she sees a bottle marked 'Drink me', she drinks. Does it never occur to her that the situations she finds herself in are dangerous, as they most assuredly are?

The Alice books are full of games rendered pointless by a complete disregard for the rules. There's the caucus race, where everyone begins to run whenever they like and in any direction they choose so that, when a halt is called after half an hour or so, everyone must be declared the winner. (I'm reminded of Phillip Adams's suggestion that all the players on the football field be given a ball to save them having to fight over just one.) A croquet match, organised by the Queen with great pomp and ceremony, instantly descends into an all-out brawl, with the furious Queen stamping about shouting, 'Off with his head,' or 'Off with her head,' and nobody taking the slightest notice. Whacking a rolled-up hedgehog with the head of a live flamingo takes croquet to new heights of savagery, yet Carroll somehow manages to make it charming. In the preface to *Alice Through the Looking Glass*, the author explains that the chess game on which the story is based 'is strictly in accordance with the laws of the game'. I'm prepared to take his word for it, although the pandemonium that follows resembles no chess game I've ever seen.

It is quite remarkable that, in spite of their complete disregard for rules and regulations, and the mayhem that results, everyone manages to get along. They bicker and fight, they contradict and undermine one another, they plot and betray, and they are completely indifferent to each other's welfare, yet somehow life goes on. The radically subversive message we might be tempted to take from this is tempered by the revelation at the end of both books that they are all just characters in Alice's dreams. They simply disappear when she awakens to find herself safely back in the kitchen, with dinner on the table and her little black kitten on her lap. Order is restored. And I suspect many young readers feel let down.

Like medieval Carnival, Alice's adventures are the temporary setting aside of normal social behaviour – a short interlude of chaos and misrule that, although liberating for a while, is not the way we want life to be all the time.

Working for our passage

On 10 December 1896, a riot broke out at the Théâtre de L'Oeuvre in Paris following the opening of Alfred Jarry's play,

Ubu Roi (or *King Turd*). It wasn't so much the shouted *'merdre'* that opened the play, although it was that too. It was more that this anarchic grab bag of schoolboy slang, puns, obscenities and bizarre goings-on made a mockery of everything decent folk held dear: not least, theatre itself (the list of characters includes 'the entire Polish Army' and 'the entire Russian Army'). Was nothing sacred? *Ubu* offended everyone (although Jarry himself is suspected of fomenting the riot). No wonder opening night was also closing night and *Ubu* was immediately banned. It drew a howl of moral outrage from the English poet and critic Arthur Symons, who derided '... the insolence with which a young writer mocks at civilisation itself, sweeping all art, along with all humanity, into the same inglorious slop-pail'. What author wouldn't kill for a review like that?

In this inglorious slop-pail, Modernism was born. Well, that's arguable, of course, but it will do for the sake of a good story. What makes the claim at least feasible is that *Ubu* so tenaciously, and uproariously, trashes almost every literary convention: Modernism being based on the premiss that you had to get rid of all the old stuff before you could impose the new stuff, even though nobody had much idea of what the new stuff would look like. *Ubu* has no dramatic structure to speak of, no character development or linguistic refinement, certainly no moral, and, for that matter, no discernible logic. If we appreciate anything about it, it will not be the incoherent plot, a crude parody of Macbeth, in which Ubu kills the King of Poland, seizes the throne, ruthlessly eliminates all opposition, then flees when the going gets tough and is attacked by a bear. Nor will it be for what the play tells us about life, since it never had any intention of saying anything about that. It will be for the way it proclaims theatrical *terra nullius*: clear your mind of everything you ever thought a play ought to be and let's all start again from scratch – with a raised finger and a hearty guffaw.

Yet, there was still quite a bit of disassembling to do first, and the twentieth century was to prove a riot of competitive cutting back, scaling down, pruning, chopping and discarding in order to minutely examine whatever scraps might be left over. In any case, tearing things down is a lot more exciting than the tedious business of building them up again. In 1910, the Italian Futurists, in one of their legion of declamatory manifestos, signalled their intention to 'Destroy the cult of the past ... totally invalidate all kinds of imitation ... Rebel against the tyranny of words: "Harmony" and "good taste" and other loose expressions ... Sweep the whole field of art clean of all themes and subjects which have been used in the past ...'. No wonder Mussolini clutched them to his bosom. Then, warming to their theme, they added this rather ominous flourish: 'The dead shall be buried in the earth's deepest bowels! The threshold of the future will be swept free of mummies! Make room for youth, for violence, for daring!'[30] – and for forests of exclamation marks.

For the Futurists, Constructivists, Neo-Plasticists and innumerable other -ists, high art was on a serious mission. There could be no room for laughter, which was firmly relegated to the low-art side of the ever-widening divide – to Krazy Kat, the Keystone Cops and Vaudeville. High-art silliness survived, but it was not meant to be funny, or at least was not *necessarily* meant to be funny.

In my youth, I found Samuel Beckett quite scary. Although I had never actually tackled him, I knew he was a 'difficult' writer and, as our English teacher solemnly assured us, a 'monumental figure in twentieth-century literature', which was quite enough to put me off. Unsurprisingly, then, at a Melbourne Theatre Company production of *Waiting for Godot* some years later, I was astonished to hear the audience laughing. Was this permitted? Wasn't *Godot* meant to be a serious work of great importance? Didn't 'monumental' mean stony-faced?

Although Beckett became progressively more self-important and maudlin as he went on, his early work has a ponderous wit of the sort that, had I known about it, would have delighted my younger self (probably more, in fact, than it delights me now).

Watt, Beckett's second novel to be published in English, is, as he confessed, an unsatisfactory book, cobbled together from various notes and fragments while he was hiding from the Nazis in southern France. The result is like one of those showily functional modern buildings – the Pompidou Centre, for instance – with all its girders, plumbing pipes and service elevators on the outside instead of being concealed behind a smooth veneer of cladding. In fact, when we do occasionally manage to penetrate the structural exterior, we find there's very little interior there. It's all plumbing.

Watt is, if you'll pardon the mixed metaphors, a thick pea soup of verbal conundrums in which we, its readers, are constantly in danger of drowning. Puzzling, infuriating and boring by turns, it is also oddly endearing. Only the (sometimes surprisingly childish) jokes, along with the elegant prose, prevent it from congealing into empty formalism, and will encourage at least some of us to persevere even when we haven't the faintest idea what's going on.

If *Tristram Shandy* never manages to get going because young

Tristram is too busy trying to record absolutely every event, no matter how trivial or irrelevant, then *Watt* never gets going because Beckett – or Watt – is forever fretting over language and its inability to make sense of experience.

Watt, a plump, red-nosed little man with a penchant for order, routine and repetition (these days he would be diagnosed as autistic), is employed as a manservant to the reclusive owner of a gloomy mansion, where he is slowly driven mad by the absurdities he encounters.

There is, for example, the vexing question of the leftovers and the dog. Watt must prepare his employer's meals twice a day – always the same disgusting sludge of fish, eggs, game, poultry, meat, cheese, fruit, alcoholic and non-alcoholic beverages, insulin, digitalin, calomel, iodine, laudanum, mercury, coal, iron, camomile and worm-powder – and he is given strict instructions that any leftovers are to be given to the dog. The trouble is, there is no dog. So Watt pays a local to bring one to the house each day. It must be kept hungry enough that it will eat the muck, but not so hungry it will die of starvation when no leftovers materialise, which is often the case. The leftovers will kill the dog before long, anyway, so a second dog-owner must be enlisted as a stand-by, and a third, and so on. Since Watt never knows if a dog will be needed or not, he has to devise an elaborate system of semaphores to let their owners know. As one difficulty is resolved, another arises, until there are so many dogs coming and going, and so many possible ways of coordinating them with the leftovers, that Watt resorts to drawing up a graph in a frantic attempt to remain in control. The more logic he applies, the more unmanageable his difficulties become. His rising sense of panic is mirrored by our own, as the situation is minutely elucidated, page after page after page, every impediment described, every alternative investigated, and every possible solution carefully considered before being discarded. It is an obsessive and exasperating demonstration of the limitations of reason, which may or may not be amusing, depending on the reader's forbearance.

Between this and that

'I am interested only in nonsense; only in that which is meaningless. Life interests me only in its most ridiculous manifestations.' This was not the most advisable line for a writer to be taking as Stalin's purges shifted into high gear, and is quite extraordinary from a man who was literally starving at the time. Daniil Kharms is one of a gaggle of Russian absurdists who emerged from under Gogol's overcoat to flourish briefly in the heady post-revolutionary days, before being summarily silenced when their political masters had a change of mind. (Perhaps it is some consolation to know that he is highly regarded a hundred years later while the moronic bureaucrats who persecuted him are justly forgotten.) Kharms goes one step further than his contemporary, Beckett, dispensing with verbal gymnastics and one-liners altogether. His silliness is pared back to its bare bones.

Language, he claims, traps the world in a straightjacket of reason, forcing us to constantly make a choice between 'this' and 'that'. But Kharms is interested in what lies between 'this' and 'that', or, to put it another way, in the clash between these two arbitrary poles. Rather than trying to transform reality, he wants to abandon the very idea of reality. For him, language has no business describing anything, and he wants his writing to be as abstract as the paintings of his friend, Kazimir Malevich. This is fascinating stuff, and noble under the circumstances, but hardly the way to live one's life. Kharms died of neglect in a grim mental institution at the age of thirty-seven; not insane, just inconvenient.

In the story 'Falling Old Women', a woman leans out of an upstairs window, curious to see what's happening in the street below. Leaning too far, she falls and shatters on the ground like glass. Another woman, hearing the commotion, leans out the window to see what's going on. She, too, falls and shatters. Then another, and another, until six women lie in pieces on the paving stones. Finally, and here's that characteristic Modernist flippancy, the narrator declares himself bored by all these stupid women falling out of windows and goes off to the market where, he's heard, a blind man has been given a knitted scarf. Many of Kharms's stories end with a casual dismissal – 'That's it', or 'I don't want to think any more'. He frequently loses interest: 'Then everyone went home,' he'll say, or 'I don't know what happened after that,' or 'I'd write some more but the inkwell has disappeared.'

Kharms's laconic nihilism is both profoundly depressing – as you might expect, given the circumstances – and grimly amusing. Although the blind man's knitted scarf is a classic *non sequitur*, the icily detached tone of the story and the narrator's insouciance are worlds away from Lewis Carroll's cloying charm. Kharms has no need to invent Wonderland. All he has to do is stand back and observe the absurdities around him, then give them that little extra twist. His genius is to be able to make *everything* silly.

In one of his tales, many of which comprise only a couple

of lines, the narrator tells us that, thanks to him, Marina Petrovna went completely bald. It sounds intriguing and we eagerly anticipate an explanation. But Kharms doesn't do explanations. 'It happened like this', he continues: 'One day I came over to see Marina Petrovna and, bang!, She went bald. And that's all.'[31] That is, indeed, all.

In Kharms's world, there is no cause and effect, nothing takes precedence over anything else, no action has consequences (at least not the ones you'd expect), and any hint of narrative development is quickly knocked on the head by a digression, an interruption, or a stubborn lack of interest (on his part). It is tempting to call this existential silliness, if that's a thing.

Anarchy in the UK

All this European high-art silliness, with its cultured undercurrent of *Weltschmerz*, was bound to take a long time to penetrate popular culture. Laughing bitterly at tyranny, death and injustice was not seemly in the lower orders, whatever they might get up to amongst themselves in the pub. What 'the people' wanted – or what they were given, anyway – was the simple, sentimental slapstick of the two-reeler. It was their duty to keep their spirits up and carry on.

To be fair, though, formalism was never going to be high on the average Joe's wish list.

Nevertheless, the erudite, narrative nonsense of Laurence Sterne or Peter Cook – which is more akin to Alice's Wonderland than the household Watt was slowly driven mad in – was bound to provoke a reaction eventually. Punk would provide the motivation and *Ubu Roi* the model.

The Young Ones, which BBC 2 bravely took a punt on in the

early eighties, brought London's alternative live comedy circuit to the small screen, where it grabbed the traditional sitcom by the throat and gave it a jolly good rogering. This is crude, violent, all-over-the-place comedy, as if all the performers are stoned out of their brains and doing whatever comes into their heads. They're not, of course, even the most chaotic scenes are carefully choreographed, but you'd never know.

The setting is a sleazy student household with an unlikely group of occupants: Vyvian is a psychopathic medical student who eats bricks and rams his head through walls; Rick an effete snob with a crush on Cliff Richard; Neil a morose hippy who lives on lentils and keeps trying to commit suicide (he attempts crucifixion several times before realising that there's no way you can hammer in that last nail); and Mike, a smooth-talker who fancies himself a ladies' man but sleeps with an inflatable sex doll. It's like Alice's Wonderland on ice (the drug, not skates).

True to its stand-up origins, *The Young Ones* is no respecter of structural integrity. Every episode is a train wreck, with the writers – Ben Elton, Rik Mayall and Lise Mayer – gaily strewing rocks and red herrings across the tracks. And when everything goes off the rails, it goes off with abandon. There's an awful lot of shouting and flailing. The already meagre plot lines are sabotaged by u-turns, diversions and abandonments, careering off into violent slapstick, surrealist fantasy, or lengthy cutaways to irrelevant scenes featuring completely unrelated characters. These last, which can occupy up to a quarter of an episode's running time, are probably the show's most daring innovation: the *non sequitur* taken to operatic extremes. It's as if we've inadvertently flipped channels. When Vyvian and Rick head to the cellar during a game of hide and seek, for example, they discover two desperate castaways on a raft in the middle of the ocean. Unimpressed, the lads go back upstairs, leaving us to watch these poor sods succumb to hunger and madness. There is nothing inherently funny about it – only its incongruity makes it so – and we are left wondering where this is meant to be leading. We should know by now that nothing is leading anywhere. As Kharms would say, that's it.

Just as Beckett and Joyce pull language apart to expose its limitations, the exuberant ferocity of *The Young Ones* effectively pulls apart the conventions of the sitcom, leaving us with shards.

The way we live now

However idiotic *The Young Ones* may get, and however many tangents the plots go off on, we always come back to these four 'types' in their London house. Whether we find them repellent, fascinating or oddly loveable, we never lose sight of who they are. All the nonsense plays out against this grounding in normality.

Sense bumps up against lack of sense, the familiar against the unfamiliar, and the laughs are in the jarring mismatch. We never cross over completely into an imaginary world with its own internal systems of logic. That's the territory of *The Maze Runner* or *Harry Potter*. Science fiction and fantasy are quite separate genres. Instead of removing us to an imagined world, silliness exposes the cracks in the real one. It toys with logic, teasing it, flirting with it and goading it, but never abandoning it altogether.

The *non sequitur*, in all its many forms, remains the simplest and most elegant way to not make sense. The very fact of a conclusion bearing no reasonable relationship to its premiss is bound to get a laugh. The obvious explanation is that it thwarts our expectations (Incongruity Theory) but that is hardly enough on its own. I suspect Dr Freud's Release Theory might have a contribution to make as well. The *non sequitur* frees us from the pressure of constantly having to maintain reason. After all, making sense all the time can be stressful, and you only have to watch the evening news to be reminded that it's not all it's cracked up to be. Anything that lets us off the hook, even just for a while, can help us take stock.

Non sequiturs have, as they say, been trending over the last decade or two, especially among young people, and especially among better-educated, middle-class young people (there's no escaping the fact that education and social status influence how we respond to humour). Situation comedies such as *30 Rock*, *Arrested Development* and *Black Books* are full of them, leaving jokes with punchlines looking a bit clunky by comparison. And that famous Old Spice ad, 'The man your man could smell like', with its delicious last line, 'I'm on a horse', is proof that a clever *non sequitur* (or, in this case, a whole string of them) can boost the sales of just about anything, provided, of course, that the nonsense never loses sight of the commercial goal.

The internet has helped popularise this particular form of silliness. It's not just that we can while away the hours watching video clips of people falling over or cats stuck in jars: in other words, it's not just the content, it's the method. Type in a subject – say, *'non sequiturs* in literature' – and you'll be offered reams of funny examples: a blog about someone's disastrous dinner date, essays on Woody Allen and George Orwell, movie clips, advertisements from booksellers and publishers, a diatribe about the weather in North Carolina, even *A History of Sanskrit Grammatical Literature in Tibet*.

The randomness of the Google search, the way one thing can lead to another that may or may not be related, has made research – and, indeed, idle curiosity – non-linear and freely associative ('If you like this, you might also like …'). We no longer demand narratives. We feel comfortable with disconnection. Increasingly, *non sequiturs* are mirroring the way we live our lives.

There are still those who insist that, if we are to cope with this weird, uncertain age, we must have more rigorous thinking, smarter ideas, more logical and scientific approaches to problems. In other words, more of what brought us this weird, uncertain age in the first place. In response, the American philosopher Ian Morton says,

> We can tidy up our ideas all we want, but the world is going to remain a fundamentally messy place that will always resist our philosophical decluttering. What we need to do instead is get comfortable with this weirdness … Even if it's true that we're really screwed,

he adds gnomically,

> let's not spend the rest of our lives on this planet telling ourselves how screwed we are. Shake hands with a hedgehog and disco.[32]

Five   WORLDS WITHIN WORLDS

The Greeks were doing it in their mosaics in Constantinople 1100 years ago, Velázquez famously did it in *Las Meninas*. But it was the French who came up with a term for it: *mise-en-abyme* (meaning something like, 'cast into an abyss').

Deconstructionists tell us that *mise-en-abyme* captures the very nature of things, the instability of meaning. None of the English equivalents – self-reference, self-reflexivity, infinite reproduction, meta-textuality, the Droste effect or 'the play within the play' – have quite the same panache as the French term, do they. None gives any indication of the fun to be had with the concept.

Like many Melbourne children, I was introduced to the Droste effect on the escalators at Myer. They were flanked on either side by mirrored walls so, as you ascended from men's underwear to bedding, you were suddenly confronted with multiple reflections of yourself, stretching off left and right as far as the eye could see. Adults, who tend to be embarrassed by seeing themselves in public, cast their eyes demurely to their feet, but for children it was a wondrous revelation of the infinite (and in Myer, of all places!). Hobart's MONA museum has a tea house made entirely of mirrors, complete with mirrored fittings, which really does make you feel that you've been cast into an abyss. Many visitors are too terrified to set foot in it, and it has now been relegated to storage.

As a literary expression, *mise-en-abyme*, while poetic, is perhaps a bit over-the-top. In suggesting the apocalyptic it can be misleading. Ironically, it is used in art and literature not to invoke the infinite, but to break down our accustomed illusions and jolt us back to reality. Look, it says, art is not some alternative world you have been transported to, it is an artefact, a fiction, or, as theorists like to say, 'a text'. *Mise-en-abyme* messes with the distinction between fiction and reality: a medieval knight in a costume drama suddenly turns to the camera and addresses the viewer; a character in a novel is writing a novel which turns out to be the one we are reading; an artist's portrait includes himself painting the very work we are now looking at (as in *Las Meninas*). There are endless examples, especially from the past fifty or sixty years, when self-referentiality has become something of a fad. The revelation at the end of the modern novel that all the foregoing was in the mind of an unreliable narrator is the pragmatic equivalent of the revelation at the end of the nineteenth-century romance that it was all a dream.

Self-referentiality tends to be treated seriously these days (think, *Atonement, The Usual Suspects, Life of Pi, Fight Club, House of Cards*). Yet it's easy to see how it might lend itself to silliness, not least *because* it is so often taken seriously. After all, if a sign refers not to some external reality but only to itself, then that is, quite literally, a loss of sense. For those of a silly disposition, the dissembling of the unreliable narrator, the shattering of comfortable illusions and the disrupting of narrative structure hold out unlimited possibilities, along with the liberties that are conferred upon a real author when he or she is able to hide behind an invented one: 'Yes, I know this is complete nonsense, but, as you can see, it has nothing to do with me.'

The Don regards himself

Miguel Cervantes is, or was, a real author hiding behind any number of invented ones, just as his most famous creation Don Quixote is an invented character who keeps threatening to become real. *Don Quixote*, first published at the beginning of the seventeenth century, fits Mark Twain's description of a classic as a book people praise and don't read. Well, nearly a thousand pages of repetitive and fairly pedestrian prose is bound to be an acquired taste. Harold Bloom is just one of many influential commentators to have declared it 'the funniest novel ever written'. Not having read every novel ever written, I can't comment, but I suspect that many modern readers are going to find it a bit of a slog. Which is a pity, really, because not only is it a key text in the Western canon, as the Harold Blooms of this world keep off-puttingly pointing out, but it will ultimately prove richly rewarding for those with time on their hands and the will to persevere.

Although *Don Quixote* is a satire, it is a delightfully silly one. On the face of it, the story is simple enough: a gaunt, ascetic Spanish gentleman, who has lost his grip on reality after reading too many romantic novels, dubs himself a knight and sets out to revive the art of chivalry, righting wrongs, defending widows and safeguarding the chastity of maidens. He recruits a farmer, Sancho Panza, as his squire. On the one hand, Sancho is sceptical and knowing – the perfect foil for his master's madness – and, on the other, a willing and sometimes gullible participant in his misadventures. (Many critics insist that Don Quixote is not mad, although anyone today who behaved as he does would be whisked away in a van.) Sancho is both the Don's protector and his dupe, as humble and witty as his master is pompous. Why such a worldly-wise fellow consents to be starved, vilified, beaten up and robbed over and over again in defence of this vain, deluded fantasist is difficult to comprehend, yet his loyalty is oddly touching.

The book begins as a relatively straightforward account of their exploits, including the famous encounter with windmills. So far, so mildly entertaining, although it's not entirely clear who is telling the story. The narrator, who may or may not be Cervantes, claims that he is simply translating a foreign text he found at his local market, and he interrupts from time to time to contradict or correct the so-called original. (To add another mirror to the reflective mix, Cervantes will later become a character, just as Don Quixote will take over the job of narrator of his own story.) It's a warning to the reader that this is going to be a journey with many twists and turns.

Over time, the Don's delusions – mistaking windmills for giants, a basin for a shiny battle helmet, his homely mistress for a high-born duchess, and, disastrously, his friends for enemies – become so entwined with reality that we, along with the people he meets, begin to lose track of which is which. At about this point I decided to give up trying to fathom all the ins and outs and surrender myself to a world in which the distinctions between fiction and fact, madness and sanity, the mundane and the fantastic, the genuine and the fake, are so muddled as to be no longer useful.

However, by now we are some 450 pages in and starting to wilt. The temptation to speed-read is almost irresistible.

Fortunately, with the beginning of Part Two things liven up. The story is richer and more engrossing and the characters more ... I was going to say 'real', but that would be to add to the confusion; more human, perhaps.

Don Quixote meets a student who tells him that a history of his exploits (meaning Part One that we have just been reading) has been published to great acclaim. This much is true: Part One of *Don Quixote* was something of an overnight sensation. As a result, the Don and Sancho, once dismissed as a couple of oddballs, suddenly find themselves celebrities, and those they encounter play along, either because they know it is in their own best interests or because they have been seduced by fame and influence (the parallels with today's celebrity culture don't need pointing out – as I am now doing). Everyone else is acting out his dreams on his behalf and the whole world has turned into a carnival of make-believe. As Cervantes scholar B.W. Ife puts it: 'When all the world's a stage, and all the men and women are playing to an audience, Quixote's bewilderment is complete: everyone else is speaking his lines.'[33]

Towards the end of Part Two, things get even weirder. The Don and Sancho visit a printery to see the proofs of Part Two coming off the presses. How is this possible? It is a bogus Part Two, written by another author cashing in on the fame of Part One, and it features a different Don Quixote. This is also basically true: one Alonso Fernández de Avellaneda did publish a spurious Part Two in 1614. For much of the remainder of the book, 'our' Don Quixote is furiously engaged in trying to prove that he is more real than the other one, despite our being reminded from time to time that what we are reading was supposed to have been translated from a Moorish manuscript found in the market.

Despite Harold Bloom's assurances, I didn't find Don Quixote particularly funny. The jokes are both cruel and infantile. What's notable about the humour of this period, Cervantes' sprawling novel being no exception, is how vicious it can be. They laughed at things then that would horrify most people today.

Yet, having worked my way through it, with varying levels of concentration, and having given myself time to digest it, I find myself in awe of Cervantes' powers of imagination and his unlimited capacity for mischief. Some 400 years before the advent of post-modernism, he had nailed all its favourite self-referential tropes.

Endless deferral

On the face of it, Laurence Sterne's forays into self-referentiality should be comparatively straightforward. Tristram Shandy is a man writing his life story. What could be simpler? Except that he is not really writing his life story, he is writing *about* writing his life story. Or, to be precise, he is writing about why he is not writing his life story. And the reason he is not writing his life story is that he is too busy writing about why he is not writing his life story. It's like the mirrored walls at Myer: an infinite regression of someone watching himself watching himself.

The more time he spends writing about his reasons for not writing his life story, the more life he has lived that needs to be written about, hence the further behind he falls.

> I am this month one whole year older than I was this time twelve-month; and having got, as you perceive, almost into the middle of my fourth volume – and no farther than to my first day's life – 'tis demonstrative that I have three hundred

and sixty-four days more life to write just now, than when I first set out; so that instead of advancing, as a common writer, in my work with what I have been doing at it – on the contrary, I am just thrown so many volumes back – was every day of my life to be as busy a day as this – And why not? – and the transactions and opinions of it to take up as much description – And for what reason should they be cut short? as at this rate I should just live 364 times faster than I should write – It must follow, an' please your worships, that the more I write, the more I shall have to write – and consequently, the more your worships read, the more your worships will have to read ... I shall never overtake myself.[34]

Needless to say, he never does. The exasperating long-windedness and the eccentric punctuation are characteristic and take a bit of getting used to.

The irony is that, in trying to discover himself by minutely recording every last detail of his life, he gets lost in a welter of irrelevancies. *Tristram Shandy*, written in an era in which individualism was increasingly being valued, is about the impossibility of knowing oneself. '—My good friend, quoth I— as sure as I am I and you are you—And who are you? said he.— Don't puzzle me; said I.' (I wouldn't be at all surprised to learn that Gertrude Stein knew about that.)

Tristram Shandy is a great big bundle of tricks, jokes and conundrums. For instance, an account of the death of Parson Yorick in Volume I is, famously, followed by two entirely black pages to signify mourning. (If there's one thing everyone knows about *Tristram Shandy*, it's the two black pages.) Chapter breaks occur, apparently at random, in the middle of conversations; there are chapters of only one or two short sentences; while one chapter (14 of Volume IX) is airily declared surplus to requirements. After a page of amiable mumbo-jumbo, he can declare, with some relief, that 'The fifteenth chapter is come at last', although, contrary to expectations, it brings nothing of much import. (This calls to mind some of *Don Quixote*'s deliberately unhelpful chapter headings, such as: 'Chapter XXIV, In which a thousand trifles are recounted, as irrelevant as they are necessary to a true understanding of this great history'; or 'Chapter XL, Regarding matters that concern and pertain to this adventure and this memorable history.')

When he gets to chapter 25 of Volume IX, Tristram feels the need to explain why a couple of previous chapters were blank, begging us not to lose patience: 'All I wish is, that it may be a lesson to the world, *"to let people tell their stories their own way"*.' Well, perhaps, to a degree, but this does sound more than a little disingenuous. Telling his story is precisely what he is not getting around to doing, as he is well aware. Anyway, the two missing chapters are duly inserted into chapter 25, which has no other content, and everything can proceed – or go around in circles – as before.

Discords and false endings

Such sophisticated literary games are, of course, all about self-identity. But a self is not always necessary. Until fairly recently, popular songs and rhymes were mostly anonymous, passed from generation to generation and owned by everyone, which is to say, no one. Although simpler than the sophisticated games of Cervantes or Sterne, their self-referencing proves that watching yourself watching yourself was not the sole preserve of the literate classes.

Silliness: A Serious History

There's a wealth of examples to choose from. Coincidentally, or not, many date from the hundred years or so following *Don Quixote*'s first publication. For instance, a jaunty little song about Oliver Cromwell's execution from this period ends abruptly with the lines: 'If you want any more you can sing it yourself/ Hee-haw, sing it yourself', which is brusquely dismissive, especially given the gravity of the subject matter. Then there's this rhyme, which mocks the people of Gotham in Nottinghamshire who had a (no doubt undeserved) reputation for stupidity:

> *Three wise men of Gotham,*
> *They went to sea in a bowl.*
> *If the bowl had been stronger*
> *My song had been longer.*

The air of finality is helped along by the fact that the last two lines clip the rhythm. In this, as in many other instances, the end of the characters means the end of the song, as if the two were synonymous: a witty conflation of fiction and reality.

A lot of fun can be had with endings. Sometimes, the nursery rhyme that announces its own ending was a way for weary parents to put off their children's demands for a story:

> *I'll tell you a story*
> *About Jack a Nory,*
> *And now my story's begun.*
> *I'll tell you another,*
> *Of Jack and his brother,*
> *And now my story is done.*

What self-respecting child would have been satisfied with such a brazen brush-off as that?

Even music can be self-referential, despite it being the most abstract of the arts. In 1772, the Hungarian prince Nikolaus I – Prince Esterházy to his friends – lingered on at his summer palace long after the weather had turned, reluctant to return to Vienna, which he disliked. Finally, his court musicians, longing for home, begged their Kapellmeister to drop the hint. Luckily for them, their Kapellmeister was Joseph Haydn, one of the musical world's greatest wits. The hint was his Symphony no. 45, nicknamed 'The Farewell'. During the final adagio, the players stopped playing, one by one, snuffed out the candles on their music stands and left the hall, leaving only two violinists to finish in semi-darkness. It was a cheeky but diplomatic gesture, and it had the desired effect. The court packed up and left the following day.

Although 'The Farewell' symphony had a practical purpose, Haydn also indulged in musical play for its own sake, and for the amusement of his fickle patron. For example, his string quartet op. 33 no. 2, nicknamed 'The Joke', doesn't know how to end. After twice drawing to a half-hearted conclusion, then unexpectedly starting up again, it suddenly pulls up short mid-phrase, as if someone has pulled the plug. The famous declamatory chord that bursts in on the sedate second movement of Symphony no. 94 – the aptly named 'Surprise' – like a bogan gatecrashing a tea party, is guaranteed to jolt awake any snoozers in the front row.

Haydn's jokes are typically at the audience's expense. People inevitably start applauding when Symphony no. 90 comes to a rousing conclusion, only to discover, after a four-bar pause, that it has started up again in a different key. At the Proms in 2005, Sir John Eliot Gardiner, conducting the English Baroque Soloists, turned and shouted, 'It's not finished!' Then the same thing happened again. So, when the work finally did come to an end, there was a hesitant silence and a few nervous giggles from those wary of being caught out a third time. Ironically, their vacillation showed they had been.

Only the knowledgeable will pick up on all the rhythmic and harmonic confusions and odd key changes that pepper Haydn's works. They have been called radical, but I don't think that's quite the right word. Was he really striving to break new ground or just having fun? It was his relative isolation at the Esterházy summer palace from the highly competitive European music scene that gave him the licence for levity. To be a prankster, it helps to be on the margins.

Mozart's *Divertimento for two horns and string quartet*, commonly known as 'A Musical Joke', was no doubt intended as revenge on those aristocrats who were elaborately praised for their amateur musical efforts while giving the young Mozart a hard time. It is full of galumphing rhythms, discord, clumsy instrumentation and other teeth-grinding gaffes. In the adagio movement, the incompetent composer Mozart is supposedly channelling has chanced upon a delightful melody that he doesn't know what to do with, so he keeps fiddling with it until it sinks into banality. The presto ends in complete collapse, as if all the musicians have suddenly fallen off their chairs. While Haydn was having a bit of harmless fun at the expense of his audience, Mozart is taking a savage swipe at his social (but not his musical) superiors.

Proving that one era's silliness can be another's high

seriousness, a number of 'A Musical Joke's comedic innovations – asymmetrical phrasing, whole-tone scales and polytonality, which would have sounded decidedly odd (and hilarious) to listeners at the time – were adopted by Ravel, Debussy, Stravinsky and others as key components of Modernism's musical language.

Inevitably, when a piece of music returns to the home key and draws to an end, thrusting us back into the real world, we experience a moment of pleasant disorientation. Eighteenth-century composers, guided by classical form, knew exactly where they were going and how they were going to get there, and everyone knew when they had arrived. The composer and critic Howard Goodall compares it to a train journey: you know your destination and arrival time and you stick to the rails, enjoying the scenery along the way. That's what made Haydn's jokey endings so startling, they derailed the train.

In the Romantic era, however, when symphonies were permitted to wander off-leash for hours on end, there was much anxiety about how to bring them to a satisfactory conclusion. One strategy (which Tchaikovsky so often adopted) was to bludgeon them to death with a sledgehammer, and the overblown Romantic finale has been providing comedians with plenty of scope ever since. Victor Borge and Anna Russell, two of the musical world's cleverest pranksters, exploited it mercilessly.

One of the funniest examples, though, is Dudley Moore's mock-serious interpretation of the 'Colonel Bogey March', which he manages to turn into a surprisingly convincing Beethoven piano sonata. It starts off sedately enough before building to a ludicrously over-the-top climax that comprises half the total length. By the end, Moore is leaping about, frenetically pounding the keys, piling crescendo on crescendo, with a look of utter desperation on his face, as if the music has taken him by the throat and refuses to be put down.

It was a bit unfair of him to target Beethoven, though, who was, after all, a master of the appropriate ending.

There was a young lady of ...

It was too hasty of me to declare in the first chapter that silliness does not respect formal structures. As with all sweeping generalisations, there is an exception: in this case, the limerick – specifically, Edward Lear's limericks, which are the very definition of rhythmic, semantic and syntactical conformity. Although Lear did not invent the limerick, which has existed in various forms for centuries (the *Three Wise Men of Gotham* is a proto-limerick, for example), he certainly made it his own.

Modern limericks tend to be like little stories, introducing a character in the first line (*A beetling young woman named Pridgets*), then informing us, in the second line, of some distinctive personal trait (*Had a violent abhorrence of midgets*). The two shorter lines that follow outline an action (*Off the end of a wharf / She once pushed a dwarf*), then comes a punchline, bringing it all to a humorous climax (*Whose truncation reduced her to fidgets*). That example, by Edward Gorey, one of the masters of the modern limerick,[35] pretty much conforms to Lear's template, with the important exception of that last line. Lear's last lines, instead of providing a surprise or a joke of some kind, double back to the first, making his limericks more self-contained. For example:

There was an Old Man of Dumbree,
Who taught little owls to drink tea;
For he said, 'To eat mice,
Is not proper or nice'
That amiable Man of Dumbree.

These days, when we get to that last line we are bound to feel a bit let down. Where's the joke, the final boom-boom? Yet this doubling back to the beginning is exactly what sets Lear's humour apart, making it one-hundred-per-cent, solid-gold silliness. Lear doesn't do jokes. He's not leading up to anything. He's not usually even telling stories. He is, rather, evoking a delicate, whimsical world of his own imagining, populated by pobbles and dongs with luminous noses and little owls who drink tea. One old man has birds nesting in his beard; another lies on his back with his head in a sack, while another dines on roast spiders and chutney. An old lady of Chertsy sits on the stairs eating apples and pears and a young lady's hair curls up a tree then over the sea. People say things like, 'Oh law! You're a horrid old bore' or 'Chickabee, chickabaw', then say nothing more. A punchline in such a setting would be boorish and clumsy. Lear's strict adherence to established literary forms, such as the limerick or the sonnet, and his simple, dogmatic rhyming schemes, help him to define the boundaries of his fantasy world and keep it from seeping out into the real one (or, more to the point, keep the real one from seeping in).

Lear's illustrations to his limericks often emphasise their circularity by using mirror images or, in the case of the owls, a lineup of identical birds, all holding little teacups, that stretches off into the distance as if they were on the escalators at Myer. The anonymity of Lear's characters (he rarely gives them names), the arbitrariness of the places they hail from ('Dumbree' is there only because it rhymes with 'tea': Dundee would have been the obvious choice) and, most of all, a rigid observance of prosody, are all designed to draw attention to form and away from content. Lear's limericks are surprisingly self-regarding.

Skaz

While *Don Quixote*'s narrator is always changing before our eyes so that we can never be quite sure who will be telling the story next (is it Cervantes, whose name is on the book's cover, the unknown Moor who supposedly penned the original manuscript, his translator, or the Don himself?), we are never in any doubt about who is telling the stories attributed to Nikolai Gogol. It's just that we don't know who he is. It certainly isn't Gogol. What we do know is that he is a charming and perceptive fellow, healthily sceptical yet tolerant, if a bit naive, and he frequently professes himself as puzzled and amused as we are by the curious goings-on he is telling us about. This is what we like about him: he appears to be one of us, assuming, of course, that we are ordinary, unexceptional people without power or influence who are just trying to get along in the world as best we can.

One thing we can say about him: he certainly gets about. Whenever anything happens, he is there. He is with the con-man Chichikov in *Dead Souls* as he falls asleep in his carriage; in 'Nevsky Prospect', he witnesses three German artisans attacking Pirogov in their shop, and agonises about being unable to find words to adequately convey their rudeness;

in 'The Overcoat', he is there to commiserate with the benighted Akaky Akakievich as he sits at his desk laboriously copying documents. He dutifully tells us all about the tailor, not because the tailor is relevant to the story of the overcoat, but because it is a convention for writers to properly delineate all characters, and it is not for him to defy convention. He knows a lot about these people: perhaps more than they know about themselves. He is familiar with their personal histories, their likes and dislikes and even what they are thinking, although occasionally certain details slip his mind. After all, it is impossible, as he despairs at one point, to get right inside a man's soul to discover everything he thinks.

Like Tristram Shandy, he finds it hard to keep up, because things happen so quickly there isn't time to note them all down. So, it is a great relief to him when Chichikov finally falls asleep, at last giving him (the narrator) an opportunity to tell us something about the man, which he has been prevented from doing until now because Chichikov has been attending balls, dealing with the town scandal-mongers, dallying with women or doing deals, all of which have had to be described.

At the end of 'The Nose', this mysterious narrator (he would appear to remain the same from one tale to the next, although it's hard to be certain) insists that he cannot understand why Kovalyov's nose detached itself from his face, later popping up in various places in the guise of a state councillor.

> And then again, how did the nose end up in a loaf of bread and what about Ivan Yakovlevich? ... No, I don't understand at all, I decidedly don't understand it! However, what's even stranger, what is the most incomprehensible thing of

all, is how authors can choose such subjects! To be honest, this is beyond all understanding, there's no doubt about it ... no, no, I don't understand it at all. In the first place, it's of absolutely no use whatsoever to the fatherland, and in the second place ... well, in the second place it's also of no use to the fatherland. I simply don't know what it is ...

Yet, all the same, despite all this, although, naturally, one or two things might be permissible, and a third thing, even ... well, when does anything make sense? ... And actually, for that matter, when you give it a bit of thought, you have to admit that there is something to all this. Whatever anyone says, such things do happen in this world – rarely, but they do happen.[36]

Well, no, they don't, actually. People's noses do not go off by themselves in search of a better life, not even rarely. Nor do dogs engage in secret correspondence (as they do in 'Diary of a Madman'). This is all just aimless blather.

The odd thing is that this fellow, always so ready to take us into his confidence, never actually materialises and the characters remain unaware of his existence. He is a persona Gogol has adopted, a narrator who, although not a character, as in a conventional first-person narrative, is more than just a disembodied onlooker. The Russians have an appealing term for it: skaz (from *skazát´*, to say or tell). It is the ironic adoption of a colloquial speaking voice whose telling of the story is part of the action of the story (a logical impossibility when the story is in the past tense). In English, Salinger's *The Catcher in the Rye* nails the tone, but the narrator is the main character, so it's not the same.

In the end, the content is less important than the rambling, characterful, *faux-naïf* and oddly lyrical style of the telling. The adoption of a narrative persona gives Gogol licence to be wildly inconsistent, to put a point of view that might or might not be his own, and to step back for an ironic, and sometimes highly critical, assessment of his own creation. When the author – or in this case, his proxy – is his own severest critic, there's not much anyone else can reasonably say.

The Irish writer, Flann O'Brien, takes skaz and self-referentiality to truly sublime extremes. *At Swim-Two-Birds*, his novel published in 1939 (the year *Finnegans Wake* first appeared) is a glorious mish-mash of Celtic myth, popular culture, comic-book Irishness, and bucket-loads of utter nonsense. It has three alternative beginnings and three alternative endings – take your pick – and the various strands of plot become so entangled that it's hard to know who's doing what to whom.

The book's unnamed narrator, an indolent student of literature who lives with his disapproving uncle, is writing a novel. So far, so familiar. But the main character of this second novel, Dermot Trellis, is also writing a novel, on the theme of good and evil.

The trouble is that neither the narrator nor his meta-fictional author are particularly skilled at keeping their creations in check. In fact, poor Trellis's characters are in open rebellion. One of them, John Furriskey, conceived by Trellis as the embodiment of evil, stubbornly insists on being a decent chap and proceeds to fall in love with Sheila Lamont, whom Trellis intended him to ravish and defile. It is left to Trellis himself, in a moment of weakness, to assault her, which results in a child named Orlick.

Furriskey and a couple of other characters discover that Trellis, their creator, can control their actions only while awake, so, with the help of a grocer's boy, they conspire to keep him sedated. 'And what did Furriskey do when he got the boy asleep?' the narrator is asked. 'Oh plenty, I said. He married the girl. They took a little house in Dolphin's Barn and opened a sweety-shop and lived there happily for about twenty hours out of the twenty-four. They had to dash back to their respective stations, of course, when the great man was due to be stirring in his sleep. They hired a girl to mind the shop when they were gone, eight and six a week with dinner and tea.'[37]

As if this were not tortuous enough, the tale is interspersed with what appear to be episodes from one of Trellis's pulp-Western novels, featuring a couple of rough boyos named Shorty and Slug, along with the adventures of the Pooka Mac Phellimey, a charming and urbane devil, and the foul-mouthed Good Fairy, who lives in his pocket.

Finally, Orlick (who, you may or may not remember, is the bastard son of Trellis, the fictional author, and Sheila, one of his characters) gathers everyone together in the Red Swan Hotel for the purpose of writing a book about his father, in which they put him on trial. This is, in effect, the novel within the novel within the novel within the novel. The hearing being a fabulously over-the-top parody of justice, it is no surprise that the poor author is found guilty and condemned by his own characters to all manner of terrible torments.

What saves all this from turning into an incomprehensible mess and compels us to persevere through the occasional longueurs is O'Brien's splendid mastery of language, a potpourri of traditional Irish blarney, a rigorous classical education, the influence of James Joyce, and the liberating effects of alcohol. He glories in obscure words and convoluted phraseology; he incorporates passages from Classical literature, school textbooks and racetrack form guides; and he gleefully subverts almost every novelistic convention. For example, although the first page is headed 'Chapter One', the whole book turns out to be chapter one, and the narrative is interrupted from time to time to provide 'a brief summary of what has gone before for the benefit of new readers', which, apart from being logically absurd, do not provide summaries at all. The contrast between the po-faced, elevated diction and the childish absurdity of what it describes is a large part of the fun. A lengthy exchange between Mac Phellimey and the Good Fairy about whether or not Mac Phellimey's wife is a kangaroo is about as silly as literature gets.

Talking to camera

On his way to the Underworld in Aristophanes' *Frogs*, Dionysus is keeping a wary eye out for murderers and perjurers. 'Oh yes, I see them now!' he cries, peering out into the tiers. It must have got a good laugh. People like being insulted, so long as it's all in good fun and not too specific, although any murderers or perjurers in the audience might have felt a pang of discomfort. In one of Plautus's plays, *The Braggart Soldier*, an errant slave makes the audience complicit in his crime, pleading: 'Folks, please don't tell Palaestrio, I beg of you,' much as characters do today in children's pantomimes. Ancient audiences, like today's, were no doubt expected to interpret this as an invitation to disobey, just to see what might happen. After all, in the land of theatrical make-believe, no actual harm could come of it.

The wonder is that this sort of thing can still tickle our fancies more than 2000 years later. We never tire of fictional characters suddenly breaking the spell by intruding into our world, especially when they do it with a knowing wink. The literary equivalent is for a character to unexpectedly address the reader, as in: 'Reader, I married him.'

When Chico Marx sits down at the piano and launches into a tune in *Animal Crackers* (1930), Groucho levers himself wearily off the settee, saunters up to the camera and says, 'I gotta stay here, but there's no reason you folks shouldn't go out into the lobby till this thing blows over.' In the theatre, the audience was at least there to talk to. On film, addressing the audience in this way raised even more conundrums about what was real and what wasn't.

Even comic strips were getting in on the act. In the twenties, Krazy Kat put his arm tenderly around the love of his life, the white mouse Ignatz, and pointed outwards: 'Look "Ignatz"', he said. 'Look at the person reading what we is saying.' They appear so vulnerable under our gaze that we feel a little guilty about reading what they is saying. Addressing the audience usually assumes authority and control, but Krazy Kat and Ignatz look as if they've been caught in the headlights.

A little over a decade after Groucho had dipped a tentative toe into self-referential waters, *Hellzapoppin* flung open the floodgates: little in cinema since has come close to matching it for sheer lunacy. The director, writer, producer and even the projectionist are all characters in their own movie, floundering around trying to work out what on earth (or, literally, what in hell, for that's where they all are) is going on. The director, in a panic, calls, 'Cut! We can't go on. Pictures have got to have a story … There never has been a picture without a story.' So the writer is hauled out of jail to provide one and the actors are expected to do their best with the little they are given. 'Oh, no, not a film within a film,' one of them whines. With apologies to the audience, they call up to the projection booth for the scene they've just shot to be played back, so we see it all again, backwards then forwards. Everything comes to a halt when the film stalls in the projector and melts because the projectionist is busy kissing his girl in the booth. This causes uproar on the set, and it's not long before the cameraman, in desperation, shoots himself. And that's just the first thirty minutes. (The rest, which falls back on its roots as a Broadway review, is a lot less inventive, despite an eye-popping dance sequence.) It never seems to strike anyone as odd that the movie is being simultaneously written, filmed and screened.

It's surprising that television was so slow to catch on. After all, home viewers were quite accustomed to being personally harangued by people flogging refrigerators and detergents, and variety-show hosts chatted to them like old friends who'd been parachuted directly into their living rooms. 'We look forward to seeing you again next week,' they'd chirrup as the credits began to roll. My aged grandmother used to take them at their word and wave back. And who could blame her? Television fostered a faux intimacy that was hard to resist. Unlike at the theatre or the cinema, where we were part of an anonymous crowd, television was one-to-one: Graham Kennedy was our friend, someone we knew and who gave a pretty good impression of knowing us.

Television drama, meanwhile, remained stubbornly self-contained. It would take a comedy to break the mould.

Basically, there were two kinds of domestic sitcom in the fifties and sixties. *Father Knows Best* and *Leave it to Beaver* were in the cloyingly sentimental group. Dad was wise, thrifty and hard-working, mum happily cooked and cleaned, and the kids were ruddy-cheeked and immaculately behaved. But, in *The George Burns and Gracie Allen Show* and *I Love Lucy* the job of the long-suffering husband was to keep his loopy wife in check and sort out the messes she got herself into. The first type was a model of how the American family was supposed to behave, the second a warning of what could happen if the little woman got out of hand. In reality, both Gracie Allen and Lucille Ball were intelligent, talented and entrepreneurial. They may have been the principal characters, and they may have had all the funny lines but, as women, they had to play dumb. Lucille Ball was apt to bawl like a baby as the disasters piled up, while Gracie was always too off-with-the-pixies to notice.

'My, the department stores were crowded today,' says Gracie. 'I was at the exchange desk and the girl was out to lunch, so we all had to wait in line ... I asked the lady in front of me what she was exchanging and she said, "I have to return these shoes for my children, they're too tight," and I said, "Well, shame on you for allowing the children to drink."' [38]

The jokes rarely get much better than this, but it's not really about the jokes. George reacts by turning to the camera and raising a quizzical eyebrow. 'You see what I have to put up with?' that look says, and we feel uneasy about being roped in and made complicit.

Complicity is behind all George Burns's monologues. At key moments, the other characters conveniently absent themselves and he saunters out onto the porch to give us his personal view of events so far, which he seems to assume we will endorse. It has the effect of putting us on his side, against his wife. In later episodes, George periodically retires to his den above the garage to switch on the television and watch along with us, to keep abreast of what's going on in his absence. There is something slightly creepy about his spying on his wife like this, although admittedly she *is* on national television, so he's just doing what we're doing. The difference is that she is implicitly aware of us watching but not of him. All the other characters have simply failed to notice George's alternative life as a real person.

We've noticed, of course, but even so, when George confides in us, it's hard to know whether he is stepping out of character or not, since the real and the fictional person seem interchangeable. In reality, George Burns and Gracie Allen were a married couple who starred in a television sitcom in which they played a married couple who star in a television sitcom. Yet, while Gracie and the others are all playing parts, George affects not to be, at least not all the time. He is a one-man chorus, simultaneously George Burns the actor and George the character playing an actor playing a character.

These days, there are so many examples of comic self-referencing in movies and television that the list could go on forever. There's the fist fight in Mel Brooks's *Blazing Saddles* spilling out into the studio where it gets mixed up in fist fights from other movies; or the characters in *Spaceballs* working out what they're supposed to be doing by watching a bootleg copy of the movie they are appearing in; or Jude Law in the remake of *Alfie*, whose most intimate and enduring relationship is not with any of the women he seduces but with us, the audience.

Woody Allen's *The Purple Rose of Cairo* also involves an actor in a film talking directly to the audience, except in this case the audience is part of the film, and the actor, who's playing a swashbuckling archaeologist named Tom Baxter, steps out of the screen into the cinema, where he meets and falls in love with a young waitress named Cecilia, who's sitting in the front row. It is an affectionate nod to the erotic fantasies of film-star fans. Later she joins him back in the movie, which has been on hold during his absence. The other actors don't know what to do with Cecilia who they can't find in the script. Further complications arise when Cecilia realises that it is the character, Tom, who loves her, not the actor playing him – an especially touching distinction.

The impossibilities multiply until they are tripping over each other. Perhaps the only way to squeeze comedy out of self-reference today is to overdo it spectacularly. But, needless to say, it all ends with Cecilia sadder but wiser.

Under the influence of French deconstruction theory, *mise-en-abyme* has recently become *de rigueur*, the *sine qua non* for any work of fiction that wants to avoid being called *passé*. As the pompous critic in Tom Stoppard's *Inspector Hound* observes, '... it has *éclat* while at the same time avoiding *élan*'. The revelatory plot twists at the ends of dramas such as *Atonement*, *Fight Club* and *Life of Pi* and the ironic talking-to-camera in *House of Cards* (the kind of thing one disenchanted critic has dismissed as 'gratuitous self-reflexive preening') are now so familiar as to be clichéd. Yet, comedians have been playing these games for centuries, mostly without the preening, and it can still get a laugh if it's done well, and to excess.

But there's one important difference: in drama, self-reflexivity is usually a startling disruption to an otherwise realistic scenario, the revelation at the end, the big surprise, something to talk about as you leave the cinema or close the book. In comedy, on the other hand, it's more likely to drive the narrative, or at least to be an integral part of it. Being a means to an end, rather an end in itself, comedic *mise-en-abyme* is apt to pass without fanfare and be accorded less importance.

Six ON AND ON AND ON

The Bible warns against it (in Matthew 6:7): 'But when ye pray, use not vain repetitions, as the heathen do: for they think that they shall be heard for their much speaking.' But battologia (needless or tiresome repetition in speech or writing) isn't always a desperate bid for attention. The heathen may have been just trying to raise a laugh. 'Much speaking' can, after all, be very funny, and the more needless and tiresome it gets (up to a point, anyway), the funnier it's likely to be.

Why use only one adjective when you have 166 at your disposal? Why settle for 'dead' to describe your parrot when you can ram the point home with 'passed on, no more, ceased to be, expired, stiff, bereft of life, off his twig, kicked the bucket, shuffled off his mortal coil, run down the curtain and joined the bleeding choir invisible'?[39] The pedant will point out that this is not repetition but redundancy: not the reiteration of the same word or phrase, but of different ones with similar meanings. Repetition is static – the same damn thing over and over – while redundancy, as in Monty Python's Dead Parrot sketch, can build a breathless momentum, giving it far more potential. The cumulative effect of endless adjectives, verbs or nouns, or logjams of redundant phrases, can take on an almost hypnotic rhythm, especially when carefully choreographed for sound as well as meaning. Samuel Beckett, with characteristic dryness, called it 'the comedy of exhaustive enumeration', and exploits it to the hilt in *Watt*.

But why is it funny? As always, a lot depends on context. An endlessly barking dog or the steady pounding of a piledriver outside the bedroom window at six in the morning are not amusing. At the very least, we have to be able to distinguish between what's a game and what's not. There's work and there's play: work is not usually funny, play often is. We need to feel that we have been invited, even permitted, to laugh, and to be confident that whatever it is we're laughing at is harmless. One of the things we learn early in life is to recognise when laughter is and isn't appropriate: a clown, yes, a dwarf trying to reach a packet of cereal in the supermarket, no. It's a lesson that, as adults, we get guilty pleasure from occasionally transgressing.

With the opening titles, *Monty Python's Flying Circus* clearly sets out its aim: this is going to be half an hour of unadulterated silliness, so let yourselves go and have a good time, confident that when the end credits roll you can slip back into your daily routines and the normal rules will be re-established. It's quite therapeutic.

In that state of grace, we can happily indulge our feelings of superiority over the raving man with the dead bird, along with the smarmy pet-shop owner, played by Michael Palin, who knows he only has to maintain his condescending grin to win the argument. There's pleasure in seeing people, especially stupid people, working themselves into a lather to no avail. Lots of comedy is based on the spiralling panic of a frustrated idiot trying to deal with a level-headed but persistent opponent: think Roadrunner, Bugs Bunny and Elmer Fudd, and dozens of other cartoon characters.

At the same time, though, there's something slightly embarrassing about the situation. As tension builds, our contempt for the man's gullibility (after all, he was stupid enough to buy a dead parrot in the first place, so a lot of his anger must surely be directed at himself, whether he knows it or not) is tempered by sympathy. His rant turns into a game of push and pull. Who'll crack first, him or us? And the longer it goes on, the tighter the spring is wound and the funnier it gets.

The Dead Parrot sketch takes an ordinary situation and, through exaggeration, makes it grotesque. It's a slightly scary reminder that the things we do every day – making a cup of tea, crossing the road, buying a bird in a pet shop – can so easily tip into lunacy. Every moment of our lives teeters on the edge of madness.

Excess, when it reaches grotesque proportions, can usually be relied on to raise a smile in the disinterested onlooker, whether it's a fat lady wolfing down a cream cake, a Chihuahua tackling a dinosaur bone or the World's Biggest Brussels Sprout (yes, there is such a thing, it's at Coldstream, east of Melbourne, it sports a cheeky grin, wears a hat and gives the thumbs-up to passing motorists). The grotesque offers release, an escape from the norm, a hint of transgression, and the unsettling combination of unfulfilled longing and fecundity. John Cleese's relentless litany of redundancies makes the grotesque theatrical, giving it rhythm, momentum and tension.

Lessons from the master

Nothing exceeds like excess, and no one does excess like Rabelais. His books are festooned with lists that go on and on, then a bit further, and then further still. He simply doesn't know when to stop. For example, a catalogue of the books Pantagruel finds in the library of Saint-Victor in Paris, although it has no bearing on the plot (or what plot there is, at any rate), fills five pages. It includes, *On the Art of Discreetly Farting in Company*; *On the use of Clear Soups* and *On decently Tippling*, by Silvester de Prierio, a Jacobite; *Three Books On How to Chew Bacon*, by the Reverend Father Provincial of Drivell; and, my favourite, *Whether a Chimera Bombinating in the Void Can Swallow up Second Intentions, as Debated over Ten Weeks at the Council of Constance*.[40]

As a sly dig at scholarship and authority, this is inoffensive enough, but Rabelais's humour could also be high-risk, as when, in a postscript to the first book, he attacks the censors who had accused him of obscenity: 'As regards their study, it is entirely taken up by the reading of Pantagrueline books, not so much to pass time merrily but wickedly, so as to harm someone, namely by articulating, arse-ticulating, wry-arse-ticulating, bumculating, bollockulating, diabollockulating, that is, calumniating.'[41] That kind of thing could get you into real strife in the sixteenth century.

Rabelais' lists are fabulously inventive. As a child, Gargantua, Pantagruel's father,

> would spew in his bowl, let off farts, piddle against the sun, leap into the river to avoid the rain, strike while the iron was cold, dream daydreams ... put the cart before the horse ... let things slip, gobble the best bits first, shoe grasshoppers, tickle himself to make himself laugh ... beat about the bush but snare no birds, believe clouds to be saucepans and pigs' bladders lanterns ... always look a gift horse in the mouth, tell cock-and-bull stories,

and many, many more.⁴² Later, as a grown man, his habits become less charming: when rising of a morning, he would '... shit, piss, hawk, fart, break wind, yawn, gob, cough, snivel, sneeze and dribble snot like an archdeacon'. ⁴³

As often as not, the plaits of verbiage are woven together for their sounds rather than their sense, thus presenting an interesting challenge for the translator. In the prologue to the third book, Rabelais tells a story about the Greek philosopher Diogenes, who lived in a barrel. One day, he rolled it to the top of a hill, where he:

> turned it, churned it, upturned it; spattered it, battered it, bent it, bonked it, dubbed it, scrubbed it, rubbed it, flattered it, banged it, beat it; bumped it, topsy'd it, turvy'd it, dribbled it, tapped it, ting-ed it; stoppered it, unstoppered it, paced it, ambled it, shambled it, haggled it; tossed it, stopped it, prodded it, shot it; lifted it, laved it, louvered it; hampered it, aimed it, blamed it, blocked it; troubled it, huddled it, splattered it; fashioned it, fastened it; walloped it, dolloped it, tickled it, tarred it, smutched it, touched it, hawked it, mawked it, hooked it, cooked it, twiddled it, twaddled it, charmed it, armed it, alarmed it, saddled it, straddled it, caparisoned it ...⁴⁴

The reason for all this frenzied activity was that Diogenes, seeing the citizens of Corinth frantically preparing for an invasion (preparations enumerated in another long list) thought he should at least be looking busy.

These absurd lists are essential to the rumbustious, uninhibited character of the writing. Later in the third book, Rabelais outdoes all his previous efforts and really lets himself go. Panurge, who has consulted Frère Jean about marriage, lets loose with a torrent of adjectives in praise of Fr. Jean's bollocks, beginning with patted, sculptured, mangled, pretty, oval, audacious and fecund; progressing to bloated, well-seasoned, cuddly, wanton and Turkish; then finishing with sibillant [sic], donkeynizing, algebraic and stallionizing. There are no fewer than 166 of them. But Rabelais is not done yet. Frère Jean counters with 169 much less flattering epithets for the bollocks of his friend, including musty, beshitten, creamed-off, pimpled, hernia'd, vainly hoping and clientless (the last two especially wounding for a man who is worried about being cuckolded).

Now, I know what you're thinking: 169 consecutive adjectives must surely become tedious. Indeed, to some extent they do. However, Rabelais employs a number of clever strategies to keep us from nodding off. One, as we've seen, is to set up musical rhythms and rhyming patterns. The Diogenes passage, read aloud, is like a piece of rap music (note, by the way, the use of commas and semi-colons to make the rhythm irregular, with a frantic gallop to the end, where we are finally brought up short by the awkwardness of 'caparisoned').

Furthermore, having lulled us with a number of similar, rather ordinary words, he will unexpectedly insert a bizarre one to give us a jolt. 'Smutched it' and 'mawked it', for instance, are meaningless. How do you mawk a barrel? They appear to be there only for their rhyme, as if Rabelais couldn't think of anything else and, in his rush, put down the first thing that came to mind. And how, we might ask, can a man's testicles be 'Turkish' when he is not a Turk? Such words are like little wake-up calls. They break the formula just when we are beginning to flag.

If that isn't enough, he sets out the hundreds of adjectives for bollocks in three columns, each with a slightly different emphasis. Read vertically, they present us with a set of similar meanings, while, if we read across from one column to another, we find more contrast.

Finally, he sets the positive against the negative. Thus, while Panurge's descriptions of Fr. Jean's bollocks are mostly generous, Fr. Jean's are withering ('withered' is in fact one of the adjectives he employs).

Rabelais pretty much milked comic redundancy for all it was worth and, until the twentieth century, few authors dared to follow him up that particular garden path.

Comfort with stimulus

Simple repetition is more common. We humans appear to have an inbuilt propensity for it. As Oliver Sacks once said, 'Our poetry, our ballads, our songs are full of repetition; nursery rhymes and the little chants and songs we use to teach young children have choruses and refrains. We are attracted to repetition, even as adults; we want the stimulus and the reward again and again ...' The trick, as writers of pop songs know, is to be able to repeat the same things over and over while making them appear fresh every time.

Children get a kick out of repeating words and phrases *ad nauseam*, testing adults' patience, whether on purpose or not. They latch onto words for their sounds and happily put them through their paces, changing them, rhyming them, refining them, combining them. Adults might find solace in the knowledge that constant repetition improves the little ones' vocabulary as it provides reassurance. As children grow older, they are told to stop being silly. They learn to be more critical in their use of words and more respectful of their meanings, with a result that their everyday language loses much of its sense of fun and experimentation. The older we get, the more functional – and duller – our language becomes.

The repetitions in nursery rhymes were an aid to memory at a time when they were passed on orally from generation to generation, often as songs. Actually, 'nursery rhyme' is a misleading term, because, as Iona and Peter Opie, editors of the *Oxford Dictionary of Nursery Rhymes*, point out, the great majority of them were not intended specifically for children. They are derived from folk tales, religious rituals, street cries, mummers' plays and songs from barrack room and tavern. So it's no wonder that many of them, with their references to death, disease and terrible violence, are scarcely suitable for children at all: or at least not for today's coddled youngsters.

Many of the nursery rhymes that have come down to us have been bowdlerised so as not to upset more delicate modern sensibilities while some, such as *Ten Little Nigger Boys* and *Little Sir William*, about the supposed ritual murder of children by Jews, have discreetly slipped from view (although Benjamin Britten bravely made an arrangement of *Little Sir William* in the 1940s).

Yet even when they survive intact, their original meanings have now largely been forgotten and the implied (or sometimes quite specific) violence of the lyrics is abstracted by the sing-song repetitions. An eighteenth-century song, which became a nursery favourite, begins:

> *We will go to the wood, says Robin to Bobbin,*
> *We will go to the wood, says Richard to Robin,*
> *We will go to the wood, says John all alone,*
> *We will go to the wood, says everyone.*

It then ekes out, over thirteen mesmerisingly repetitive verses, a surreal tale about the killing of a giant bird. Apparently, it was originally sung by hunters on their way home from the day's slaughter, but you wonder if some of them weren't driven mad by it. I'm reminded of a running gag in an episode of the BBC series *The Fast Show*. It begins with a group of happy hikers setting off along a mountain track singing, 'Val de ri, val de rah, val de ri, val de rah, ah, ah, ah, ah, ah, ah', over and over. As they wilt, their singing wilts with them. Finally they are stumbling along mumbling incoherently, except for one indefatigable chap bringing up the rear, who is still lustily belting out the chorus. Mustering their last reserves of energy, they beat him to death with their alpenstocks.

The following rhyme, probably from the nineteenth century, is pure silliness, a list of absurd (or what we would call surreal) incompatibilities. This is the sort of nonsense Edward Lear was fond of. The repetition of 'I saw' at the start of every line – a variety of repetition known to linguists as anaphora – pulls the disparate elements together to provide some sense of coherence:

> *I saw a fishpond all on fire*
> *I saw a house bow to a squire*
> *I saw a parson twelve feet high*
> *I saw a cottage near the sky*
> *I saw a balloon made of lead*

I saw a coffin drop down dead
I saw two sparrows run a race
I saw two horses making lace
I saw a girl just like a cat
I saw a kitten wear a hat
I saw a man who saw these too
And said though strange they all were true.

A Rose is a rose is a rose

'We all know that we should never ever ever, fiddle around in any way with electrical devices. Never.'[45] This is good advice, if a tad overemphasised. In his children's books *A Series of Unfortunate Events*, Lemony Snicket tries to give Rabelais a run for his money, the difference being that the master's endlessly variegated redundancies are here straightforward repetitions. Children love this sort of thing, not only because it is gloriously excessive, and certainly not because it is good advice, but mainly because it parodies the way their parents talk to them. Parents, like the ancient heathens, think their much-talking will make them heard.

In the ninth book of the series, *The Carnivorous Carnival*, chapter five begins with a description of déjà vu. On the next page, there is the start of chapter five again, almost (but not quite) word for word. In a similar vein is: 'He found himself reading the same sentence over and over. He found himself reading the same sentence over and over. He found himself reading the same sentence over and over.'[46]

Repetitions, as distinct from redundancies, rarely get any

more sophisticated than this, which is why they are usually restricted to children's books and popular songs. They occur a lot in rock music, both in the music itself and the lyrics. The same head-banging chord over and over, with a shouted 'Yeah, baby, yeah, yeah, yeah, yeah, yeah' can be hypnotic, or, if you're Frank Sinatra, infuriating. In his grumpy later years, he complained about rock music's 'almost imbecilic reiteration'. The fade-out at the end of many pop songs suggests that the repetitions go on forever.

In any case, a century earlier, the French composer Eric Satie had already pushed musical repetition to its logical limits. His *Vexations* from around 1893 is a piano piece, which bears an ambiguous notation suggesting that it be repeated 840 times. Nobody took this seriously until John Cage arranged a performance in New York in 1963 (there's always someone, isn't there – and it's usually John Cage). It took a relay of pianists over eighteen hours, and the (no doubt apocryphal) story goes that when the final chords were struck, a drunk at the rear of the auditorium, who had wandered in to get out of the cold, rose unsteadily to his feet and shouted, 'Encore! encore!'

What qualifies *Vexations* as silly, as the drunk in the back row instinctively understood, is not the repetition as such: all composers use the repeat mark. It is the ridiculously excessive number of them, and, of course, Satie's vexatious intent – while we might find the idea of it amusing, it would have been excruciating to sit through, and apparently only one tenacious soul did, presumably to prove a point rather than because he was enjoying himself. Sometimes the idea is enough, and there is something ploddingly didactic about Cage's determination to spell it out.

After a certain number of repetitions (not many, actually), it becomes clear that the tune has yielded up whatever it had to offer and it slowly dawns on us that nothing else is going to happen and we are faced with the same thing over and over, without variation or development. This is the point at which it becomes amusing, when we realise it's all a tease. But it won't be long before boredom, then annoyance, set in as the tease turns into torment. There's only a brief interlude of comedic opportunity between when we wise up to what's going on and when we decide that, okay, we've got the message and it's time to shut up.

This goes to the heart of the problem: how to deploy repetitions – or redundancies – so as to convey the idea of boredom and exhaustion without sinking into boredom or exhaustion. This is not so much of a problem in a written text because, if the worst comes to the worst, the reader can simply skip an eye across the line and take in all the repetitions as a block. We don't need to read every one of Lemony Snicket's 'ever, ever's to get the picture, we just need to know there are far too many of them, and that's the funny part. But if a mother were reading this passage to her children, she would have to introduce some theatrics – a sigh here, a gasp there, some slowing down and speeding up – to give it enough variety to maintain her children's interest and show that she was sharing the joke. The hilarity would largely depend on her performance.

Rabelais's interminable redundancies work in much the same way. While we might be tempted to speed-read (because they can, admittedly, become tedious at times), we know that if we do we might miss a little gem inserted surreptitiously amongst the hordes of banalities or, worse, fail to grasp the subtle architecture on which his lists are constructed. There are variations, even if there's no development. The question is, how much tedium are we prepared to endure in order not to miss out on the occasional witticism?

As Rabelais understood, the trick to maintaining our interest is to stretch the comedic interlude and keep the laughs coming for as long as possible. He doesn't always succeed – five pages of successive adjectives is pushing it a bit, even for him – but he is generally pretty good at holding tedium at bay.

Marge Simpson, opening a new concert hall in Springfield, panics when people start leaving during the opening bars of Beethoven's Fifth because they don't think it's as good as the ring-tone version. 'Wait,' she cries. 'After interval we'll be presenting a new work by Philip Glass.' With that, the audience rises as one and stampedes for the exit. Cruel, perhaps, but a reminder that there is only so much monotony most of us are prepared to put up with.

Yet, people came back week after week for *Little Britain*'s endlessly repeated catch-phrases – the only gay in the village, computer says no, yeah-but-no-but-yeah, and so on. *Little Britain* can make Philip Glass's monotony seem positively baroque by comparison. The moment the scene opens on a bright-eyed young couple facing a bank manager across a desk, we know exactly what's coming: 'Sorry,' she intones, shaking her head forlornly, as if it had nothing to do with her, 'computer says "no".' It's funny the first few times because it crystallises the kind of abnegation of responsibility we suffer all the time at the hands of anonymous bureaucrats. There's a welcome feeling of release when something unpleasant or infuriating that we feel powerless to do anything about is made to look ridiculous.

And there's just enough variation between one sketch and the next to keep us engaged. After a while, though, we begin to wonder whether the writers have simply run out of ideas. As the variations start to look more and more contrived, the humour drains away.

So, why was the show so popular? Why did the same sketches go on long past their best-before date? Perhaps because constant reiteration of the over-familiar provided comfort – a feeling of security and dependability in unpredictable times. Whether we admit it or not, most of us are like dogs: we want interesting new things to happen only within very narrow limits and only so long as they won't upset our expectations. Most of us thrive on routine.

Groundhog Day – a movie that takes routine as its subject – suffers from the opposite problem, with so much variation within a supposedly repetitive framework that it would appear to be undercutting its own premiss. TV weatherman Phil Connors (Bill Murray), who is in Punxsutawney, Pennsylvania, to cover Groundhog Day festivities, finds himself (for reasons that are never made clear) condemned to relive the same day over and over. This doesn't sound like a very promising set-up. Most films, unless they happen to be *Last Year at Marienbad*, are careful to avoid repetition for fear of boring the audience. As it turns out, however, Phil's days are anything but repetitive. He soon realises he can do whatever he likes without consequences. He binges on food, spies on people, robs them and insults them, knowing that tomorrow he'll be back where he started and none of it will have happened. He tries suicide by taking a bath with the toaster and driving off a cliff but always wakes the following morning to find everything just as it was. Changing tack, he learns to play the piano, becomes a talented sculptor, an expert on French poetry and a local hero, until all ends happily when he finally wakes up to find that at last he has crossed over into the following day.

The paradoxical upshot is that Phil's days are more exciting and incident-packed than they would otherwise have been. So presumably this is not meant as a satire on the repetitiveness of daily life so much as a moral warning about the dangers of living without limits. Yet, Phil appears to be having a whale of a time (even killing yourself is a lark when you know it's not going to be fatal), so maybe that's not it either. In one telling scene, he sits chatting to a couple of locals in a bar. 'What would you do if you were stuck in one place and every day was the same and nothing you did mattered?' he asks. 'That sums it up for me,' one of them replies matter-of-factly. But, of course, it is not their story the film is interested in, because that would be truly repetitive.

A slip of the tongue

Repetitions help us to remember through pattern, rhythm and predictability. This can be very handy, whether we're reciting Homer from memory (not that anyone does that any more) or singing a comic song. Repetition oils the wheels of recitation.

However, it can be turned to the opposite purpose. The devilishness of tongue twisters is that they employ rapid repetition of similar sounds to court chaos. But they are not just a tongue problem. Consonants and vowels are usually grouped together according to how they are articulated by the tongue, lips and larynx. Using high-resolution brain imaging, some American researchers have discovered that each of these groups is controlled by a different area of the brain. Why this should be so is one of God's little secrets. As long as those different areas are working away in an orderly sequence, there should be no problem, which is why language is structured the way it is, with equitable distributions of the various consonant and vowel sounds so as not to overtax our grey matter. When we get into a muddle, however, is when we have to deal quickly with a string of sounds that are generated by the same part of the brain.

Sibilance is trickiest. A string of 's' and 'sh' sounds, as in 'She sells seashells by the seashore' or 'Sinful Caesar sipped his snifter, seized his knees and sneezed' (from *Singing in the Rain*) can be a real test, more so if you throw the occasional 'th' sound into the mix, as in: 'The sixth sick sheik's sixth sheep's sick.' I'm told that there are finger-fumblers as well – phrases that, although not necessarily difficult to say, can get signers into a terrible tangle, and for much the same reason: larynx muscles or finger muscles, they're all the same to the language-generating brain.

We don't confuse vowels and consonants because they come from very distinct brain areas. For the same reason, people who stutter don't have any trouble when singing. Furthermore, vowels are less likely to cause difficulties than consonants, perhaps because they don't make many demands on the tongue or lips. There's a little dialogue I learned as a child that does involve a bit of vowel-play, along with a lot of 'm' sounds: a woman takes her saucepans to the blacksmith to be mended (that's how old it was even then). 'Are you copper-bottoming 'em?' she asks, to which his reply – 'No, I'm aluminiuming 'em ma'am' – provides a vigorous lip workout.

Making sense isn't a high priority for tongue twisters, of course, although we do expect at least a modicum of comprehensibility. The fun is in the verbal gymnastics, bumping up against our limitations and being forced to confront the fact that something we always assumed was second nature is, in fact, nigh-on impossible. They present us with a conundrum, seeming to defy common sense. In this way, tongue twisters are sobering revelations that we're not quite as clever as we thought we were.

It would appear that tongue twisters are a generic part of human makeup, as old as language itself. They are known to have been popular in ancient Greece and Rome, for example, where they were used to teach children to distinguish syllables. Punctuation was non-existent and words in both Greek and Latin were often run together without breaks, which no doubt offered many delightful opportunities for misinterpretation. Tonal languages, such as Mandarin Chinese, present almost unlimited scope. There's an example on the internet that runs together sixteen almost identical words that make sense only when said aloud, enunciating the tonal differences: sì shì sì/ shí shì shí/ shí sì shì shí sì/ sì shí shì sì shí. Lots of lovely sibilance there! It means, simply: 4 is 4/ 10 is 10/ 14 is 14/ 40 is 40 – which sort of makes sense.

Our brains are wired for forming certain sound combinations that are inherent in whatever language we speak. An English speaker would not normally have any trouble distinguishing 'l' and 'r', for example, but, as Stephen Fry once said, the quickest way to drive a Japanese insane is to ask him to say 'crimson-lipped fritillary' (it's a variety of lily). No doubt a Japanese speaker could come up with something to drive Stephen Fry insane.

As always, a hint of smut will spark things up. A remarkable amount of eighteenth-century humour depends upon phrases or sentences that are all feigned innocence on the surface but turn smutty when mispronounced (a technique adopted more recently by the Two Ronnies). It's a cunning stunt. I have no idea whether the Pheasant Plucking Song is eighteenth-century or not – its origins are obscure – but, in any case, it is a fine example of the genre.

> *I'm not the pheasant plucker,*
> *I'm the pheasant plucker's mate*
> *And I'm only plucking pheasants*
> *Cos the pheasant plucker's late.*

There are many verses, and every line of every verse involves pheasants and plucking, so getting safely through to the end is a truly remarkable feat.

Given that tongue twisters are meant to be said aloud, it's odd how rarely they pop up in film, television and radio. One of the best-known examples is a 1932 BBC recording of a Cicely Courtneidge sketch in which the frightfully upper-class Mrs Spooner orders two dozen double damask dinner napkins from a department store. Tossed back and forth between her and the two shop assistants, the phrase goes through every possible permutation – 'two dizzen dipple dummest danner nipkins' and so on – until finally, in desperation, she settles for twenty-four serviettes.

After Rabelais

I first read *Finnegans Wake* as a young man, long before I'd read anything else by James Joyce. I wanted to be able to boast that I had read the famously 'unreadable' novel (although my friends remained stubbornly unimpressed). For nearly three years, on and off, I sat with the Faber paperback edition in one hand and William Tindall's *Reader's Guide to Finnegans Wake* in the other, wending my way sentence by sentence through its labyrinths of language. What kept me going were the jokes. As an editor once told me, most readers are prepared to put up with a lot of punishment if they think a joke is coming. *Finnegans Wake* is a very funny book once you get used to it. I'm glad I made the effort when I did because I am sure I would not have the stamina now. This is a novel made up almost entirely of riddles, parodies, reversals, puns, invented words, 'quashed quotatoes, messes of mottage'. It is, in the words of its author, 'the hoax that joke bilked'. There is no plot to speak of, and no beginning or end. *Finnegans Wake* finishes mid-sentence so that we have to circle back to the top of page 1 to complete it (a technique known as recursion, employed in several well-known folk songs). Theoretically, one could go on reading it forever. It's the central conceit of the novel that history is not just one damn thing after another but an endless cycle, with cultures moving through divine, heroic and human ages before beginning all over again. If *Ulysses* is Homer's *Odyssey* re-enacted in a single day by a modern Irishman, *Finnegans Wake* is the endless cycle of world history dreamt during a single night by another.

Repetition is at the heart of it. Just as our world is made up of a set number of elements, so Joyce's dream world is made up of a set number of key motifs endlessly rearranged and recombined. Like carnival-goers on a ferris wheel, we keep revisiting things we have passed before, seeing them in a different light each time.

This, you might protest, is heroic, even pretentious, rather than silly. But on this solid foundation, Joyce builds airy castles of ludic fantasy, which is what first attracted me to him. While every pun and mangled phrase has a host of hidden meanings, we don't have to get ourselves into a sweat over them. This is, above all, a farce.

Like Rabelais, Joyce is fond of lists. For example, H.C. Earwicker, pub-keeper and the dreamer of the book's dream, is accosted by one Herr Betreffender, who blows Quaker's oats at him through the keyhole and threatens to break his head if he doesn't get a drink. Betreffender's insults start off simply enough – Informer, Old Fruit, Goldy Geit and so on – gradually becoming more inventive (I cite at random): Yass We've Had His Badannas, Tight before Teatime, Unworthy of the Homely Protestant Religion, O'Reilly's Delights to Kiss the Man behind the Borrel, Left Boot Sent on Approval, Plowp Goes his Whastle, Ruin of the Small Trader, Man Devoyd of the Commoner Characteristics of an Irish Nature, Woolworth's Worst, Easyathic Phallusaphist, Guiltey-pig's Bastard, Fast in the Barrel, Boose in the Bed, Mister Fatmate, and more than ninety more.[47]

While Herr Betreffender's names for Earwicker are abusive, a corresponding list of epithets for his wife, Anna Livia Plurabelle, in chapter five is more complimentary, an echo of Rabelais's trick of pitting negative lists against positive. Among those that happen to tickle my fancy are: Peter Peopler Picked a Plot to Pitch his Poppolin, A New Cure for an Old Clap, E'en Tho' I Granny a-be He would Fain Me Cuddle, What Barbaras Done to a Barrel Organ Before the Rank, My Skin Appeals to Three Senses and My Curly Lips Demand Columbkisses, Mum

It is All Over, To Keep the Huskies off the Hustings and Picture Pets from Lifting Shops, and so on. [48]

Joyce's lists are more cerebral than Rabelais's yet, in a way, sillier, in that they appear to have abandoned all pretence at referentiality. These names have escaped the bounds of what a name is supposed to be. Paradoxically, that tends to make them less funny than Rabelais's, which, for all their madness, rarely lose sight of what they describe. While Rabelais always appears to be having a whale of a time, Joyce can come across as trying too hard. A friend of mine says the Joyce of *Finnegans Wake* reminds him of a child rushing downhill on his bicycle with his hands off the handlebars, shouting, 'Look at me! Look at me!'

What Rabelais's and Joyce's lists have in common, though, is their efflorescence. Words and phrases tumble uncontrollably, one on top of another, growing and expanding until they take on a life of their own. They rollick, romp, tease and dazzle, building into an unstoppable avalanche of mental pictures, half-baked notions and misapplied references. You have to give yourself over to them, revelling in their excess, happy just to lean back and enjoy the ride.

Beckett's lists have the opposite effect. They entrap every idea, thought and action in a thick, static web. While Rabelais is the archetypal Trickster, Beckett is a curmudgeon. The unrelenting reiterations in *Watt*, which are likely to go on long after our patience has run out, rehearse all possible approaches to a given situation until no course of action seems possible. On the one hand this, on the other hand that. And so on and so on. Paul Auster said that the narration of *Watt* seems to be strangling itself.

There is, for example, the question of who made Anne Lynch

pregnant, which led to her death and that of her newborn twins. Every contender is painstakingly considered, although given that the reader is given very little idea of who Anne is (for Beckett, as for Joyce, words are more interesting than people), it all seems a bit academic. Some believe Bill is to blame, some, Joe, and others, Jim.

> And of those who had been in agreement, many were now in disagreement, and of those who had been in disagreement, many now were in agreement, though some that had agreed agreed still, and some that had disagreed still disagreed. And so new friendships were formed, and new enmities, and old friendships preserved, and old enmities. And all was agreement and disagreement and amity and enmity, as before, only redistributed.[49]

And around and around we go, until eventually we get off the merry-go-round to find ourselves more or less where we got on, if a little dizzier.

Not all of Beckett's repetitiveness is so entertaining. Some of it is tedious, which is presumably as he intended it to be. He is deliberately, even maliciously, testing our patience.

It was the repetitiveness of *Waiting for Godot* that made the audience laugh in the production I saw all those years ago. 'Let's go,' says Estragon. Vladimir replies, 'We can't.' 'Why not?' 'We're waiting.' 'What for?' And we've anticipated the answer. It's a catchphrase, just like 'the only gay in the village' and 'computer says no'.

But enough of high-seriousness. Steering a course back to the ludic leads us across the geographical and cultural divide to the USA and the effortless lightness of Abbott and Costello.

'Who's on First' may well be the most popular comedy sketch ever. It began in Vaudeville before moving to radio in 1938, then film, then television. Now it is on YouTube where, the last time I looked, it had scored well over eleven million hits. Not bad for a single routine. It is still very funny, and so much a part of American folklore that chunks of it can be quoted without acknowledgement – most recently in Jim Jarmusch's film, *Paterson* – on the confident assumption that everyone will recognise it.

This sort of quick-fire sparring had been a staple of vaudeville for generations before Abbott and Costello got hold of it, and the running joke depends on our acceptance that Who, What, and I Dunno might be people's nicknames, which is a big ask. But we're sure to forgive.

Abbott is coaching a baseball team and Costello innocently asks him the players' names. Someone called Who is on first base, What is on second, and I Dunno on third. It's not hard to see where this is headed:

> Well then, who's on first?
> *Yes*
> I mean the fellow's name.
> *Who.*
> The guy on first.
> *Who.*
> The first baseman.
> *Who.*
> *The guy playing.*
> Who's on first.
> *I'm asking you who's on first.*

That's the man's name.
That's who's name?
Yes.
Well, go ahead and tell me.
That's it.
That's who?
Yes.
...
What's the guy's name on first base?
What's on second.
I'm not asking you who's on second.
Who's on first.
I dunno.
He's on third. We're not talking about him.

This is Beckett played entirely for laughs (and a decade earlier, moreover). There's the same repetitiveness, the same circularity, the same relentless exposure of language's shortcomings, even the same play on the name What or Watt. But, of course, the effect is entirely different. Needless to say, Abbott and Costello didn't win the Nobel Prize but, at the same time, Beckett has a long way to go before he scores eleven million YouTube hits.

'Dave's not Here', a masterly little two-hander by Cheech and Chong, has the same relentless inevitability, but this time with a slow, stoner lethargy. It begins with a knock on the door. Dave has scored, but he thinks the cops are on to him. He needs to get inside fast. But his unnamed mate is too bombed out to know what's going on.

Who is it?
It's me, Dave, open up, man, I got the stuff.
Who is it?
It's me, Dave, man, open up, I got the stuff.
Who?
It's Dave, man, open up, I think the cops saw me comin' here.
Who is it?
It's, it's Dave, man, will you open up? I got the stuff with me.
Who?
Dave, man, open up.
Dave?
Ya, Dave, c'mon, man, open up, I think the cops saw me.
Dave's not here.

Dave gets more and more wound-up in the face of a brick wall of incomprehension. It's the classic emotional-whirlwind-meets-stoic-resistance scenario we get in the Roadrunner cartoons and the Dead Parrot sketch, but with the roles reversed so it's the supposedly smart one who ends up losing it.

How long is too long?

Whether repetitions or redundancies make us laugh or bore us to tears depends on our mood and the circumstances. Some people will find Joyce's lists of names hilarious while others will be left completely cold. When we do get a kick out of them it is, in part, because they take us back to the simplicities of childhood and the language games we once played. Whenever we want to sound childlike and indulgent, we need only to double-up on a word. If 'poo' is too direct, saying 'poo-poo' makes it more acceptable (if a bit twee). Someone who is good is admirable, but a 'goody-goody' is offensively good. 'Car-car' and 'choo-choo' turn impersonal machines into personalities. As far as I'm aware, this doubling of words to soften and infantalise them is common to almost all languages.

Once repetitions take on Lemony Snicket dimensions and begin to test our limits, the pleasure we get from the build-up of tension turns positively erotic: the expectant hush as the cork is slowly prised from the champagne bottle before it shoots across the room with a loud bang and a fountain of froth. The longer the build-up can be drawn out, the funnier it will be. Provided, of course, that it isn't drawn out too long, so the tension is allowed to dissipate.

Yet, how long is 'too long'? How do we know when the tension will dissipate? Of all the various forms of humour, repetition is the most difficult to explain, the hardest to get right, and the least predictable. When Sideshow Bob steps on a rake in *The Simpsons* and hits himself in the face, that's mildly amusing, but the writers decided to have him do it again and again to make it funnier. Just for interest, they continued until the humour drained away, then doggedly pressed on until it became funny again. Sideshow Bob steps on rakes for a full ten minutes. Had he kept going even longer, it would have once more turned unfunny.

As Americans like to say, go figure.

Seven GETTING OUT OF HAND

Things fall apart

The scene: a suburban house under construction. The central front door is flanked by symmetrical window openings. The front porch, supported by perky wooden columns, is almost complete. With a little more work, this will soon be a neat, compact, respectable-looking bungalow.

A truck laden with window frames drives up and two builders climb out. One is stout, the other thin. The owner of the house promises them $500 if they can finish the job by next Monday. The men are Stan Laurel and Oliver Hardy.

This is not going to end well.

From the moment they climb out of the truck, they are bickering and sniping. They get in each other's way and trip over things, the truck rolls backward, tipping the window frames onto the ground. A sign outside the building next door says 'Hospital QUIET', and a policeman is standing guard. Laurel and Hardy get to work. They hit their thumbs with hammers, fall off ladders, swallow nails, and step on the ends of planks which spring up and whack them on the back of the head. A nurse emerges and asks the policeman to keep the noise down. He gets hit in the face, tripped up and covered in paint. The nurse is pushed backwards into a trough of wet plaster. Both are reduced to quivering wrecks. Oblivious, Laurel and Hardy soldier on. Finally the owner returns to find that, miraculously, the house has been completed, so he hands over the $500. At that instant, a small bird lands on the chimney, causing it to collapse and sparking a chain reaction. Windows start popping out, the porch falls down, the roof caves in. The owner angrily demands his money back. During the ensuing brawl, what remains of the house is reduced to rubble. The End.

Finishing Touch, made in 1928, might not be one of Laurel and Hardy's greatest efforts, but it conforms to a familiar pattern: inept innocents blunder into a scene of order and stability and reduce it to chaos. The Marx Brothers exploited it, as did Harold Lloyd, Charlie Chaplin and, more recently, Lucille Ball and Mr Bean. It exposes the way established systems are vulnerable to anything new and unpredictable. Russian authors loved it. Chekhov's one-act farces typically begin with a chance remark or gesture being taken the wrong way, which leads to situations spiralling hopelessly out of control, with devastating consequences. Yet, it is no accident that the heyday of the comedy of entropy was the first few decades of the twentieth century, and that its medium of choice was the silent movie.

Unlike radio shows and novels, which are limited to describing funny situations or recording funny dialogue, the movies can show people actually doing funny things, free of the constraints of language, unmediated and apparently spontaneous. It works so well that, even after the advent of the talkies, comedies about everyday situations spiralling out of control often remain dialogue-free. Chaplin, for one, continued to make what are essentially silent films (such as *City Lights* and

Modern Times) well into the 1930s; for all her garrulousness at other times, Lucille Ball was usually struck dumb when things got out of hand and panic set in; both Benny Hill and Mr Bean were masters at letting the action tell the story. It's much funnier to watch order collapse than to be told about it. Language can sometimes get in the way.

Early one- and two-reelers (roughly from 1912 to 1920) were little more than strings of exuberant sight-gags: athletic, inventive and delightfully crazy, although, it has to be admitted, a bit predictable after a while. Slapstick is slapstick and it hasn't changed much over the centuries. In the 1910s, movies were serving up a feast of frantic chases, outwitted cops, fluttery-eyed girls (who, *in extremis*, were just as capable of swinging a brick at a villain's skull as the men were), morally outraged matrons and runaway Model Ts careering through brick walls into swimming pools. Spectacular automobile accidents were a favourite, a reminder that, whatever modernity's benefits, it was not without pitfalls. The earthy exuberance of these ten- or twelve-minute shorts, their simplicity and the surreal madness of their threadbare plots, milked the possibilities of an exciting new medium to the full.

To pick a random example, *A Busy Day* (1914) opens with Chaplin in drag as a blowsy, argumentative dame sitting among the spectators at a street parade. With its well-drilled soldiers marching in step and its immaculately trained horses, the parade is a perfect symbol of order against which the inevitable mayhem will play out. Seeing her husband trot off after a pretty girl, the woman jumps up in a rage, and in no time at all is kicking policemen, pushing people over, jabbing a bowler-hatted gentleman up the rear with her umbrella and generally leaving a trail of disaster. In one especially funny scene, we see her flying across the screen in a flurry of petticoats as the soldiers march solemnly past in the opposite direction. At the end, she is thrown off a wharf and left blindly thrashing about in the sea. So, what was that all about? There's no plot, no character development, no overt moral purpose, no sense: this is rollicking, comic-book violence.

Without words, character development is necessarily limited. The humour must be physical. (Caption cards are rarely used to deliver jokes: Keaton and Chaplin didn't like them and kept them to an absolute minimum.) The Little Tramp, Steamboat Bill jnr. and Harold Lloyd's bespectacled go-getter are incapable of learning from experience. They don't plan or anticipate, just respond instinctively to whatever comes their way. So, inevitably, they keep making the same mistakes. When Chaplin (in *His Trysting Place*, 1914) gets annoyed with the slurping of the burly man next to him at a cafe counter and idly flicks soup in his face, he should know what he's asking for. Yet he looks quite put out when the man responds with a slap. Instinctively, he slaps back. They sit there slapping one another for a while, then they ramp it up, punching and kicking. One by one, the other patrons are drawn in, the cafe owner is knocked out and furniture is destroyed. When the place is in ruins and everyone is on the floor, Chaplin pulls himself together, puts on his coat and walks out with an air of complete indifference. Whatever modern urban life might throw at you, and however inept you might be in dealing with it, luck will see you through in the end, provided you keep your dignity. No wonder Chaplin appealed so much to the Russians.

He once said that all his films were based on his getting

himself into trouble while doggedly insisting on being a proper little gentleman. 'That is why, no matter how desperate the predicament is, I am always very much in earnest about clutching my cane, straightening my derby hat, and fixing my tie, even though I have just landed on my head.'[50]

By the twenties, Chaplin, Keaton, Lloyd, Laurel and Hardy and a few other big names, had been given increasingly generous budgets and progressed to making features. This allowed them to slow the pace a little, taking time to develop characters and stories. The slapstick is still there, but it is no longer the film's *raison d'etre*. As one critic has said about Chaplin's most enduring creation, the humour doesn't come from the Tramp bumping into a tree, but from his lifting his hat to it in apology.

The longer format gave Chaplin leave to indulge his instinct for social reform. His silliness is often more purposeful and reflective than silliness ought to be. He mixes (some might say dilutes) comedy with large dollops of Dickensian pathos, and his sentimentality, which so endeared him to audiences at the time, will strike many of us today as mawkish.

Meanwhile, the more hard-headed Keaton was undertaking ever more complex and expensive projects. *The General* is a Civil War comedy–drama of extraordinary ambition. It cost nearly half-a-million dollars to make, quite a sum in 1926. Although it is full of spectacular physical stunts (including a real locomotive plunging off a burning bridge), *The General* is not without its moments of delicately surreal silliness. A cheeky undermining of audience expectations comes towards the end when, in the midst of battle, Keaton commandeers a cannon. As he lights the fuse, the barrel lurches back so the ball shoots vertically into the air. Keaton stands peering skywards for a while, he steps to one side, then the other, then wanders off. The cannon ball never does come back down.

Laughing and gasping

As anyone who has ever ridden on a roller-coaster knows, there is a link between laughter and fear, although, like the connection between laughter and violence, it's not easy to pin down. Both laughter and fear spring from incongruity and transgression, but does laughter express a submission to fear? Is it, instead, a way of gaining power over it (as in the pop-psychologists' advice to 'laugh away your fears')? Or is it an attempt to re-establish emotional equilibrium after a scary experience?

Keaton's astonishingly acrobatic stunts in *The General*, which amount to a catalogue of all the life-threatening things you can do on a moving train, are funny because their scariness is undercut by his casual indifference, as if he – or rather, Johnnie Gray, the character he's playing – is dumbly unaware of the risk. We can see he's risking death, and Keaton the actor knows *he* is, but Johnnie Gray remains blissfully unaware. Whether perched precariously on the cow-catcher swatting railway sleepers off the tracks, accidentally skewering enemy soldiers on the battlefield, or embracing his sweetheart at the end of the film, his demeanour never changes. Johnnie is a little island of unflappable determination in the middle of a whirlwind.

In the days before CGI, the pranks could be dangerous. When Laurel and Hardy (in *Liberty*, 1929) engage in a bit of rough-and-tumble on the girders of an unfinished building, the street far below them hasn't been edited in later, since nobody knew how to do that. They really are slipping and sliding around twelve storeys up. (There are nets beneath them, out of shot, but even so.) And, when Charlie Chaplin is accidentally locked in a lion's cage in *The Circus* (1928) and one of the huge beasts fronts up to stare him straight in the eye, the terror on Chaplin's face is not acting.

Steamboat Bill Jnr (1928) includes Buster Keaton's most incredible feat of daring. Dazed by a hurricane, he stops in the street to get his bearings. Suddenly, the front wall of a two-storey building falls forward over him. Miraculously, he emerges unscathed because his body is perfectly framed by an open window. No fakery was involved. It was almost suicidal, and the cameraman is said to have covered his eyes as the two-ton wall came crashing down. The window frame was just big enough to allow Keaton two inches of clearance on either side. Although Fatty Arbuckle had employed the same stunt some years before, it was a canvas stage-flat that fell around him. Keaton's version is far more impressive, of course, but does the risk make it funnier? We might be so busy gasping that we forget to laugh. What *is* funny is his laidback reaction. He simply steps over the rubble and hurries off.

Admittedly, the most famous silent-movie escapade, Harold Lloyd's hair-raising suspension from the hands of a clock high above the traffic in *Safety Last* (1923), was elaborately faked, yet it was still risky.

Even today, some people will find *Safety Last* more scary than funny. We will chuckle nervously in anticipation as he begins to clamber up the stone wall of a city office building, fingers and feet awkwardly grappling for purchase. We guffaw when, about halfway up, he is covered in birdseed and besieged by pigeons. We shriek when he grabs the rope that's been thrown to him only to find it hasn't been secured at the other end. We gasp when he gets entangled in netting, hold our breaths as he dangles precariously from the slowly-detaching minute-hand of a clock, then, when he finally struggles to the top and we let our guard down, thinking it's all over, we suddenly let out a scream when he hits his head and totters drunkenly along the parapet. From a modern perspective, it all goes on far too long, but Lloyd's hapless everyman is very easy to identify with and the carefully managed ratcheting-up of tension keeps us gripped to the bitter end. Although not exactly laugh-a-minute, it's no less exhilarating than a roller-coaster ride.

Slapstick talks!

With a limited menu of physical gags at their disposal, the silent film stars had a job keeping the laughs coming, so vast was the number of comedies being made. People just couldn't get enough of them. Harold Lloyd alone made nearly 200 short films and, at one point, Chaplin was churning out one a week. One way of dealing with the problem was to make the gags ever bigger and more elaborate. By 1922, being chased by a policeman was old-hat, but being chased by the entire Los Angeles Police Department, as Keaton is in *Cops*, restores the fun. The long-shot of the lonely little fellow running down the street with a horde of uniformed men in hot pursuit is both hilarious and poignant, especially when you know that the crimes he's committed – stealing a house-full of furniture, knocking out a traffic cop, throwing a bomb at the mayor's daughter, and setting off a fire hydrant in the middle of a police parade – were entirely unintentional.

Excess isn't always so rewarding, though. Laurel and Hardy's *Battle of the Century* (1927) is the apotheosis of the custard pie fight, the assumption being that if one custard pie in the face is amusing, then 3000 (that's the number claimed, although 300 seems more likely) must be uproarious. Whether you agree or not will depend on your mood, as well as your patience.

As everyone must surely have known at the time, the balloon had to burst eventually. People can't just go on punching and kicking and throwing things at one another without some waning of interest, even if the ambition does keep inflating. As it happened, the talkies pretty much pulled the plug on visual slapstick, and a lot of the silent stars were left stranded. Even Chaplin struggled. Some had unattractive nasal twangs, others failed to appreciate that maniacally waving their arms around didn't qualify as acting any more, or that the simple storylines demanded by silent pictures looked a bit clunky in the age of sound. To top it off, the cumbersome recording equipment severely restricted freedom of movement. The talkies were not just silent movies with dialogue added, they were a whole new genre. Film comedy had to be rethought.

While the silent stars were struggling to adapt, the Marx Brothers barged right in and made themselves at home. After more than twenty years' experience in live theatre, they had verbal patter down pat. In fact, their first two movies were straightforward adaptations of their Broadway hits. The verbal sparring flows relentlessly on like a mountain river, one punchline tumbling over another, so it's all we can do to keep up. If you miss a joke, then never mind, you'll be hit with another before you even realise. Marx Brothers's dialogue has the rhythm of rap. If this sounds sophisticated today, in the early thirties, just a year or two after the talkies were invented, it was dazzling.

Getting Out of Hand

In *Animal Crackers* (1930), for example, Groucho, flanked by two women, asks them, apropos of nothing,

> 'What d'you say, are we all going to get married?'
> 'All of us?'
> 'All of us.'
> 'But that's bigamy.'
> 'It's big of me, too. It's big of all of us. Let's be big for a change. I'm sick of these conventional marriages: one woman and one man was good enough for your grandmother, but who wants to marry your grandmother? Nobody, not even your grandfather.'[51]

Groucho and Chico will pursue a line of comic banter wherever it takes them, like distracted beagles following a scent, until it dawns on them that they've gone too far down the wrong path and suddenly snap back to where they are supposed to be. Chico, with his phoney Italian accent, will mishear a word – 'why a duck?', for example, instead of 'viaduct', and ask, 'Why a duck? Why no chicken?' Instead of correcting him, Groucho will take the baton and run with it. 'I don't know why no chicken. I'm a stranger here myself', and together they will weave an intricate tapestry of nonsense from one simple misunderstanding.

It's as if the apparently intuitive leaps from one gag to the next are leading the plot. But if they are, they are leading it astray. Marx Brothers's plots tend to be a tangle of loose ends. Not that we're likely to mind: after all, nobody watches a Marx Brothers movie for the plot.

Unlike Chaplin or Keaton, who remain always the centre of attention, the brothers are three very different but complementary individuals, more or less of equal status, although Groucho tends to dominate through sheer force of character. (Actually, there are four of them if you count Zeppo, the straight man, or indeed five if you count the inestimable Margaret Dumont, who serves as patsy in all their best films.) So the humour is multi-layered and eclectic. Several unrelated things are likely to be going on at once, with Groucho's acid insults competing for attention with Harpo's lecherous fumblings and Chico's frantic efforts to keep control. Our eyes are sent dancing all over the screen.

There's a scene in *A Day at the Races* (1937) that perfectly illustrates the technique, although any number of scenes would do as well. Dr Hackenbush (Groucho), an incompetent vet posing as an even more incompetent doctor, has been hired by a financially strapped sanitarium. He is examining a wealthy patient, Mrs Upjohn (the long-suffering Margaret Dumont), who has high blood pressure on one side of her body and low blood pressure on the other. Dr Steinberg, a real doctor, has turned up in the hope of exposing Hackenbush, but is immediately buried under a torrent of insults (not, it has to be said, among Groucho's most inventive). Harpo and Chico, in white 'surgical gowns' borrowed from Joe's Service Station, are introduced as Hackenbush's colleagues. The sanitarium's manager stands by, looking lost throughout. To begin with, there's a flurry of farcical handwashing, then some equally farcical introductions, with everyone bowing and genuflecting at random. Pointing to the patient, Steinberg shouts, 'Take her pulse,' so Harpo grabs her purse. ('He doesn't spell very well,' Groucho explains.) When three nurses arrive, Harpo, leering maniacally, puts one of them into a headlock and has to be wrestled away. Her dress is torn off in the melee and she runs out screaming. Meanwhile, Mrs Upjohn has been upturned on the examination chair and is skidding around waving her feet in the air. Harpo lathers her up with shaving cream while Groucho scrambles after her, furiously polishing her shoes with a surgical gown. In a desperate attempt to restore order, Dr Steinberg calls for X-rays, prompting Chico to dart forward shouting 'X-rays, X-rays' like a newspaper vendor, while a grinning Harpo scatters X-rays gaily across the floor. There's so much chaos and noise we hardly notice Dr Steinberg getting hit in the stomach and falling backwards into a basin of water. Six people are on-screen at once, all at odds with one another and each one out of control. Finally, Harpo gleefully sets off the overhead sprinklers and they rush for the exit.

All this takes just over four minutes: it's extraordinarily economical. And, although the mayhem might seem, at first glance, to be random, the steady ratcheting up of the pace is choreographed to perfection.

Raising psychopaths

The silent comedians, however badly they might have behaved, were nearly always gentlemen at heart. The Marx Brothers are anything but. American society had changed. The thirties were a tough decade, and Chaplin's brand of naive optimism wasn't going to cut it with those on the breadline. The Marx Brothers don't just have things happen to them, they deliberately cause mayhem and, having set it in train, they keep gleefully plugging away until everyone and everything has been brought to ruin. A lot of disillusioned Americans at the time must have wished they could throw around insults with Groucho's panache, that they could be as blasé, cutting and in control.

For completely unguarded nastiness, however – destructive, vindictive, bad-tempered, no-holds-barred malice – the cartoon provides the perfect vehicle. By replacing people with animated drawings, cartoons can indulge in the most egregious savagery with impunity. Theirs is violence without consequences. Censors in the thirties, so intent on weeding out any suggestion of sexual impropriety, didn't seem to notice.

Watching real people getting clobbered or putting themselves at risk is bound to elicit audience sympathy. This is what makes *Safety Last* so gripping. We're human, after all. In the neo-Cartesian world of cartoons, however, pigs, rabbits, cats and wolves are immune to pain and fear. As a result, when Felix the Cat scales the wall of a tall building, there will be no empathetic gasps or squeals from the audience.

Hence, while the Marx Brothers were tip-toeing around the Production Code, Bugs Bunny was settling every difference of opinion with the aid of a shotgun, on the dubious assumption that the children laughing along were not going to develop into psychopaths.

To be fair, Disney's violence was as nothing compared to that of his competitors, Hanna-Barbera, Warner, Fleischer and MGM. The cartoons they made for television in the fifties and sixties are orgies of pitiless revenge. Plots are non-existent and the characters do little else than dream up ways of inflicting physical injury on one another. There is something hypnotic about the single-mindedness of it all.

Children's cartoons were far more brutal than anything on television for adults. But then perhaps children had the greater need. Not for nothing is the setting so often a picture-perfect suburban bungalow with a picket fence, a neat front lawn and lace curtains at the windows: middle-class order and stability which, for many disaffected youngsters, must have seemed ripe for a bit of anarchy. When a small, powerless creature such as a mouse or bird comes up against a large, predatory one, it's not hard to guess who's going to triumph. Of course, it wasn't that children wanted to do away with their parents – who'd cook dinner and pay for summer camp? But it was nice to fantasise. That's why there's never any blood, and getting flattened by a steamroller or swallowing a live hand grenade causes no permanent damage.

All the same, given that violent behaviour was presented as being innocuous and so much fun, a lot of previously wholesome youngsters must have come away with the idea that the best way to deal with people they didn't much like was to shoot them.

Although *I Tawt I Taw a Puddy Tat* is a recent adaptation of a 1950 Warner Brothers cartoon, it has all the elements that make it representative. This is, in effect, an eloquent summing-up of what American cartoons are all about. Sylvester the Cat is trying to infiltrate Granny's upstairs apartment, where Tweety-Pie the canary sings happily in his cage by the window. That's the sum total of the plot. Sylvester is just doing what comes naturally to him – trying to get a meal. Yet, we are expected to cheer Tweety on as he slams a window down on Sylvester's paws, pushes him off a high window ledge, topples a kitchen dresser onto him, burns him on a hot stove, hits him in the face with a frying pan, electrocutes him, sucks him into the vacuum cleaner, smashes him into a brick wall, pushes him off the window ledge a second time onto the road far below where he is run over by a truck, cheers Granny on as she pummels him with a broom, then a baseball bat, and then, to top it all off, drops a piano on him.

All this in little more than three minutes, and the whole time both the bird and his victim are gaily singing the title song in two-part harmony. A moment before Sylvester is crushed by the piano, Granny joins them for the final chorus.

What on earth are we meant to make of this gaudy concatenation of gaiety, camaraderie and murderous brutality? Why is Sylvester so persistent? There must be easier catches. Why is he so unnaturally cheery and forgiving in the face of the terrible things being done to him? And, incidentally, how does a canary lift a piano? More to the point: why is the clearly demented bird being touted as the good guy?

These are stupid questions, of course. Logic has nothing to do with it. Insofar as this violence is unmotivated and completely pointless, it is the very essence of silliness. It has a raucous, Rabelaisian gusto, like some infernal abstract ballet. To judge by the comments on YouTube, some people find it a hoot, and a remarkable number say that it takes them back to the happy days of their childhoods. Surely they can't all be psychopaths.

The misfit against the machine

In the heyday of the Hollywood B movie, if you wanted to create tension, you might conspire to have your heroine strapped to a conveyor belt bearing her inexorably towards a whirling circular saw blade or some other grisly instrument of mutilation. Although everyone knew she'd escape, they couldn't wait for the next Saturday's matinee to find out how. There's something especially compelling about someone being delivered into the jaws of death by conveyor belt. There can be no reasoning with its unrelenting momentum, no appealing to its better nature, no possibility of give and take.

When cartoon characters find themselves in this situation, as often happens, they will scramble free at the last minute and take off in the opposite direction, legs spinning like whirlwinds. Can they outrun the belt? Probably, although it's touch and go at times as their energy flags and they begin to lose ground. Oddly enough, they never think to jump off the side.

For a laugh without a scream, you might leave some hapless amateur in charge of a conveyor belt in a factory, then slowly ramp up the pace, causing havoc as brute mechanics take control. Either way, it's human fallibility against inhuman consistency. The first scenario is inherently dramatic, the second, because it doesn't court death or injury, is comedic.

In *Modern Times*, Charlie Chaplin is employed to tighten bolts on unidentified metal components as they stream past on a belt. Two men further up the line hit them in with hammers, then Chaplin, with a spanner in each hand, gives them a jaunty twist. At first all goes well. Then human frailty intervenes. Having paused momentarily to scratch his armpit, he has to race to catch up. A fly buzzes around his head, he sneezes, his supervisor yells at him, he has an altercation with his co-workers (inevitably; Chaplin is always having an altercation with someone). Meanwhile, the components keep trundling blindly past. The more he tries to restore order, the more out of control everything gets and the faster the conveyor belt seems to go. He ends up spreadeagled on the belt, clinging for dear life as he disappears through the hatch, not into a whirling saw blade, but enmeshed in the gearing. The machine has literally consumed him.

When he finally knocks off, he can't shake the mechanical rhythm out of his bones. He staggers around, still clutching the spanners as if they are part of his anatomy, performing an awkward little bolt-tightening dance. He has a playful go at tightening his co-workers' noses, and the nipples of a passing woman. Now, in a sense, he has consumed the machine.

Without this rather touching coda, the conveyor-belt scene would be no more than a commentary on the dehumanising effects of modern technology. But Chaplin's absorption of the factory's repetitive tempo and his transformation of it into dance suggests some kind of reconciliation. At the very least, he keeps his individuality, remaining an amiable misfit. The ambiguity makes *Modern Times* more than just social satire.

Ambiguity wasn't Lucille Ball's strong suit. After all, American television in the fifties was hardly the place for it. Nor was she much concerned about social satire, except for her love of chaos. Her reinterpretation of Chaplin's conveyor-belt scene is pure farce. But farce with a human face.

Lucy is the archetypal frustrated housewife, constantly trying to make it in show business, despite a demonstrable lack of ability. Throughout *I Love Lucy*'s long and hugely popular run (it went through several incarnations, and remains one of the most successful sitcoms in American television history), she and her Cuban band-leader husband are at loggerheads, he expecting her to stay at home and she determined to branch out. If that makes it sound formulaic and conservative, *I Love Lucy* mostly manages to avoid the trap. Although she makes a terrible hash of whatever she attempts, Lucy's daffy brand of anarchy unintentionally undermines whatever system she is trying so desperately to negotiate, and, when everything ends in pandemonium, only one or two old grouches seem to mind. Even Ricky, her husband, is forgiving.

There are several internet sites devoted to Lucille Ball's facial expressions – happy, miserable, surprised, horrified, quizzical, dazed and bewildered, you name it. One critic has called her 'rubber-faced', which doesn't sound particularly flattering, although I'm sure he meant it well. A related site, ironically entitled 'Buster Keaton's facial expressions', makes the contrast explicit.

The silent film comedians are all bodily action. That's how they express themselves and suggest character. At the conveyor belt in *Modern Times*, Chaplin darts back and forth, wriggles, jumps up and down and waves his arms about. He's like a jack-in-the-box. Yet his face remains inert.

Lucy's face, though, is always the centre of attention. We are never in doubt about what she's thinking. Even as she is borne aloft by a bunch of balloons, or engulfed in dough during a baking contest, or slides off the roof while trying to install an aerial, or accidentally foils a bank robbery, creates mayhem as the world's most incompetent flight attendant, or sets fire to the kitchen, the comedy lies less in what's happening than in her reaction to it. Stunned bewilderment, withering contempt, childlike innocence, exaggerated delight or horror: it's all in the eyes and the way her mouth drops open in wordless surprise. *I Love Lucy* was one of the first sitcoms to be filmed (rather than going to air live), and an unprecedented three cameras were used, making creative editing and close-ups possible.

When Lucy and her friend Ethel are employed to wrap chocolates on a conveyor belt, there can be no doubt about what's going to happen. We've been here before, and much of the humour comes from the anticipation. The fearsome supervisor, a woman with a voice like a megaphone, issues a stern warning that if even one chocolate gets to the packing room unwrapped, they'll be fired. She makes it sound like a capital offence: the comedic turn always being more effective when thrown into relief by the supporting characters taking themselves too seriously. Naturally, they start out well. 'This is easy,' Lucy beams, which is the signal for things to begin spiralling out of control. The chocolates turn from inert objects into malevolent little beings. Before long, she and Ethel are stuffing them into their mouths, down their dresses and into their hats, anything to get rid of them. Remarkably, though, they stay seated. There's very little body movement. The comedy is in the anxious glances, the rapid breathing and the wide-eyed panic.

When she returns, the supervisor, failing to notice the bulging cheeks, overstuffed hats and guilty expressions, booms, 'You've done well,' then calls up to the operating room, 'Speed her up!'

For all her rollicking, rumbustious pranksterism, Lucy made slapstick up-close and personal. If the Marx Brothers reinvented comedy for the talkies, Lucy rejigged it again for television. People sitting in their living rooms with their TV dinners on their laps and the dog at their feet demanded intimacy and her facial gymnastics convinced them that she was performing just for them.

Post-silliness

These days, when a computer in Silicon Valley knows our taste in music, and robots are taking over our jobs, the mechanical seems the least of our problems. It's algorithms we have to worry about, even if most of us neither know nor care what an algorithm is. How odd that most of the time we are quite accepting of artificial intelligences telling us what to do and how to do it. We even accept the term 'artificial intelligence', which, for our grandparents, would have been the preserve of nightmarish science fiction. Digital technologies admonish us, patronise us, manipulate us, confer praise or blame, bully and cajole us, while carefully monitoring our every move. Yet, we don't seem to mind, at least not until someone in Bangladesh gets hold of our credit card details. Today, it would seem, everything is permanently out of control, and we've learnt to live with it.

It's a situation begging for comedy, but how to do it justice without falling back on satire or parody? How to fully embrace the nebulousness of the post-everything world?

In episode eleven of *Arrested Development*'s second season (2004–2005), the nerdy son, Buster, after an argument with his mother, goes for a swim in the ocean, fully clothed (it's a long, oedipal story). Someone shouts, 'Lucille! Watch out for Lucille!' and, thinking this is a reference to his girlfriend, Buster ignores it. A moment later, his hand is bitten off by a seal that's been turned loose in the ocean. Later, the surgeon causes much confusion by telling the family that Buster is going to be alright. What he means is that the left hand couldn't be saved, so Buster will be 'all right'.

Jokes like this just don't work. They are really, really dumb. They can't even begin to justify their elaborate set-ups. Nobody's going to shout 'loose seal' to a swimmer in danger, nor would any doctor say a patient was going to be 'all right' unless he meant 'OK'. *Arrested Development*'s writers know their gags are dumb, of course, which is why they keep them coming. They are a tease. And they take us right back to the Marx Brothers's 'Why a duck?'.

The Indonesians have a term for this: *jayus*, meaning a deliberately lame joke that elicits good-natured amusement rather than irritation because of its playfulness. The ability to treat an idiotic remark as a *jayus* is considered a sign of wisdom and generosity.

Arrested Development's humour is of a completely different order to that of *30 Rock* (2006–2013), Tina Fey's more-or-less concurrent series for NBC. Both shows are grounded in realism and both start from a clichéd premiss. *Arrested Development* features a dysfunctional family trying to revive its fortunes, and *30 Rock* is about a variety-show writer torn between temperamental performers and an egotistical network executive. (Oh, no, not a show within a show!, to paraphrase *Hellsapoppin*). But, from these over-familiar starting points, they take off into flights of surrealist lunacy, albeit in quite different directions. Like the Marx Brothers's movies, they are confused, frantically paced, and completely unhinged, a heady mix of physical and verbal humour. But, instead of beginning with order and having it gradually spin out of control, these shows are permanently out of control, on the understanding that order is an illusion anyway. Everyone is disrupting everyone else. There is no stabilising centre – no 'straight man' figure of the kind Margaret Dumont provided for the Marx Brothers.

30 Rock's gags are funny. Some of the best are given to Jack, the network executive (Alex Baldwin): 'Lemon, you look terrible, and I once saw you eating oysters while you had a cold'; or, 'Do you know what family means to me? Resentment, guilt, anger ... Easter-egg hunts that turn into knife fights.' Meeting a woman for the first time, the nervous head-writer, Liz Lemon (Tina Fey) says, 'One time at a summer camp I kissed a girl for a dare, but then she drowned.' And one of the fictional show's stars, the self-obsessed Jenna, recalling her girlhood ambition to be a cheerleader, says that her mother told her there were only three things standing between her and success – her breasts and wanting it badly enough.

Some geek with nothing more constructive to do has calculated that there is an average of 9.5 jokes every minute, which, although a completely meaningless statistic, sounds entirely plausible. Just Google '*30 Rock* best jokes' and you'll find reams of them.

You'll have less success with '*Arrested Development* best jokes'. The sites are there, of course, but they don't provide jokes as such, but rather descriptions of absurd situations. There's a definite paucity of punchlines. *Arrested Development*'s humour comes from an ironic undermining of humour. Or, to put it another way, it's funny because it is so determinedly, and so childishly, against humour.

Yet, despite their differences, what makes *30 Rock* and *Arrested Development* so emblematic of their time is that their silliness is not an add-on to a conventional storyline, but systemic. Every aspect of every episode is inherently silly. And deeply cynical. Finding themselves in a world that is no longer comprehensible, in which reality seems to have slipped away, they shrug their shoulders, throw up their hands in surrender and say, 'What the hell!' If you're treading on thin ice, you might as well dance.

Banging the gavel

It's hardly surprising that the law has been a favourite target of satire, parody, mockery and good old-fashioned piss-taking ever since Moses handed down the Ten Commandments. The courtroom scene is a comedic staple. A remarkable number of them involve animals, for the simple reason that a dog or a cow giving evidence is inherently funnier than a mere human, and can make the humans appear even stupider than they are. The famous trial in Aristophanes's *Wasps* is initiated by a coddled domestic dog who has accused a stray mongrel of stealing cheese from his master's house. Among the several kitchen utensils called as witnesses is a cheese grater, who admits under questioning that, while employed as a quartermaster, he grated cheese for the troops. This has nothing to do with anything, and the mongrel's prospects look grim, until someone has the bright idea of bringing forth his puppies, whose piteous whining reduces the prosecutor to tears. 'Enough, enough,' he shouts. 'Step down! Step down! ... It's this damned soup. I knew it was a mistake. I'd never have started weeping like that if I hadn't been bloated with soup.'[52] For sheer unbridled silliness, this can hardly be bettered, and I would love to have seen it on the Greek stage, with actors colourfully done up as dogs and cheese graters.

Trial scenes, whether dramatic or farcical, were a favourite with Renaissance playwrights, too, being a great way to highlight the gap between lofty codes of behaviour and base human self-interest, all within the context of a familiar order of events in a familiar setting where everyone has an established role to play. So, when things go wrong, as they inevitably do, the entire fabric can unravel in spectacular fashion without the audience losing sight of who's meant to be who. The comic courtroom scene presents us with the starkest possible contrast between order and anarchy.

Corrupt or incompetent judges struggle to keep control, malicious prosecutors cast procedure to the wind, witless defendants haven't a clue what's going on, and confused jury members look on in dumb disbelief. Trials typically end in uproar, with the accused getting off (this is, after all, comedy we're talking about) not because the system works, but after some surprising and unlikely intervention, such as the mongrel's puppies and the soup. At the end of Flann O'Brien's *At Swim-Two-Birds*, the fictional author's trial by his own characters is cut short when they decide there's been enough talk and drag him out to the courtyard for 'half a minute with the razor', but that's unusually harsh. Peter Cook does a wonderfully deadpan impersonation of a biased judge summing up for the jury: 'We have heard, for example, from Mr Bex Bissell – a man who by his own admission is a liar, a humbug, a hypocrite, a vagabond, a loathsome spotted reptile and a self-confessed chicken strangler. You may choose, if you wish, to believe the transparent tissue of odious lies which streamed on and on from his disgusting, reedy, slavering lips. That is entirely a matter for you.'[53] John Cleese, who can't remember whether he's council for the defence or prosecution, respectfully lodges an objection when the judge pulls out a gun and shoots the defendant in the witness box. Shakespeare, Lewis Carroll, the Marx Brothers (in *Duck Soup*) and countless others have all had a go at the courtroom scene, and it is far from exhausted yet.

Gleeful disgust

The British love gore, the grosser, messier and more irksome the better, although not until moral codes were relaxed in the seventies and eighties could its full comic potential be milked. *The Young Ones* is a feast of gleeful disgust – the mascot on Vyvian's car is a severed human leg that looks as if it's been hacked off with a blunt knife. After an argument with Rick, he spends most of one episode with an axe lodged messily in his head. Why this sort of thing should be more characteristic of English silliness than that of other countries is a moot point. The Germans, Russians and French don't usually find bodily fluids and mutilation hilarious. Even the Spanish, who have always done a good line in the visceral, tend not to play it for laughs. Only the Americans, unsurprisingly, have latched on to it with enthusiasm, even coming up with a name for it: gross-out comedy.

American gross-out is relatively light-hearted and effortless. The American tradition of slapstick violence, going right back to nineteenth-century burlesque and Vaudeville and peaking with Sylvester and Tweety, provides a good grounding – just add blood.

The Farrelly Brothers' movie *There's Something About Mary* is a master class in comic aggression, the torture of small animals and the spilling of semen. It knows its genre and exactly how to work within it, and develops believable characters to carry it off. In one memorable scene, Mary asks Ted to let Puffy out of the bathroom, but the heavy pounding on the bathroom door is ominous. 'What kind of dog is Puffy?' he asks nervously. 'A border terrier, like Benji,' she calls back sweetly. Sure enough, little Puffy is sitting on the bathroom floor, a picture of innocence. But, as Ted bends down to say hello to the 'cute little fella', Puffy lunges, fastening onto Ted's face like the extraterrestrial in *Alien*. Locked together in combat, they skid into the living room, flailing around on the floor as Mary and her over-tanned mother look on in horror. An exotic bossa nova provides an incongruous accompaniment. Puffy drags Ted across the floor by the leg, crunches his ear, then clamps his teeth firmly into his crotch. Ted is spinning around the room screaming, with Puffy clinging to his vitals like a kid on a fairground ride. Ted slams Puffy against the furniture, gouges his eyes and pummels him with ferocious karate chops, but the dog won't let up. After a tense standoff, with Ted unwisely goading the incensed little mutt, Puffy launches himself across the room, Ted ducks and the dog shoots out the window. There's a breathless pause before we hear him crash into the garbage tins far below. This is not the end for Puffy. He will suffer further indignities later in the film, but, of course, he will emerge unscathed, as he must.

It's all pure cartoon slapstick, but with real people and a (supposedly) real dog. The editing, the choreography, the perfect balance of believability and preposterousness and, not least, the bossa nova, rub together in a grotesque parody of the musical–comedy dance sequence. It takes skill to make people laugh at the inherently repugnant. *There's Something About Mary* is the Farrelly Brothers at their breeziest.

For the English, on the other hand, gross humour looks more like a gritted-teeth revolt against traditional prudery and good manners, so it is usually more laboured. This kind of thing just doesn't seem to come as naturally to them.

Consider this, for instance. A young soldier lies in the dust under a hot North African sun. One of his legs has been blown off and the stump spasms and oozes. A passing peasant girl kneels solicitously beside the groaning man ('It hurts, it hurts!'

he cries) and cradles his head in her lap. 'Aw, never mind, luv,' she chirrups, in a broad Cockney accent, 'just run it under the cold tap.' This is the warped world of Richard Lester's *How I Won the War* (1967). Lester was never one for subtlety. Yet he remains one of cinema's masters of silliness. In fact, *How I Won the War*, like Lester's earlier film with the Beatles, *A Hard Day's Night*, is so relentlessly silly it becomes exhausting. Lester is one of those rare souls thrown up from time to time by the English class system whose sense of humour is unaffectedly and amorally childlike.

Without wanting to get too grandiloquent about it, I wonder how much of this rather determined up-yours to accepted standards of taste is a product of national disillusionment. Maybe you have to have lost an empire. Only after a fall from grace is a nation free to blow raspberries at its own former pomposity, and the likes of *Blackadder* and *Horrible Histories* can let loose with ridicule that earlier generations would have found treasonous. It's striking how many British sitcoms of the past fifty years or so, from *Hancock's Half Hour* and *Steptoe and Son* to *The Office*, *Extras* and *Detectorists*, are about failure. Because the British have fallen from such great heights so decisively and so fast, their self-mockery seems especially pointed and self-lacerating.

Not to mention endearingly infantile. When the defiant, yet utterly incompetent Black Knight, in *Monty Python and the Holy Grail*, is hacked to pieces until all that's left of him is a limbless torso spurting blood ('All right, then, we'll call it a draw,' he calls, as his assailants walk away without a scratch), what are we actually laughing at? Partly, I suppose, at a grotesque exaggeration of the sort of deluded optimist we are all too familiar with. But might it also be our disbelief that anything so grisly is being presented to us as comedy in the first place? The Pythons are throwing down the gauntlet – laugh at this if you dare – like naughty children continually testing their parents' tolerance. Unfortunately, like children, they are apt to go too far. A television sketch about live organ transplants, in which some poor sod is pinned to the table in his own living room while his liver is cut out with a bread-knife because his organ-donor card doesn't stipulate that he must be dead, is more gore than wit.

Perhaps these scenes are especially irksome because the Pythons usually come across as being so civilised, with their learned jokes about Aristotle hitting the bottle and the All-England-Summarising-Proust Competition. Cutting out livers and mashing up hamsters are more *The Young Ones'* territory. After all, that's what being a punk is supposed to be all about, isn't it? From the Pythons, though, it's a bit like hearing your dear old granny say 'fuck'.

Beyond the custard pie

The origin of food porn is the custard pie in the face, which Laurel and Hardy and the Three Stooges took to a peak of choreographed excess. Pie throwing is both erotic (they are not creamy *custard* pies for nothing) and shamefully wasteful, which is why it doesn't work when the pies are obviously fake. Unlike, say, throwing a pot of paint at someone, it will dent the victim's dignity without causing physical harm. The intent is playful. When news cameras catch Bill Gates or Rupert Murdoch glowering out through a face-full of yellow goo, it can be smugly satisfying, but really, these days, a bit ho-hum.

Silliness: A Serious History

These days we want to test the limits of disgust. And, when it comes to food, those limits are pretty narrow. Many years ago, as part of a live 'happening' by a group called The Sydney Front, one of the actors pulled a spoon and a can-opener from the pocket of his overcoat and, casually delivering a nonsensical monologue, ate a can of Pal. The effect was unaccountably repugnant. There's nothing actually wrong with eating dog food. Although probably not very appetising, unless you're a dog, it's unlikely to do any harm, so long as you don't make a habit of it. It can't be any worse than a meat pie. So why was everyone so repelled?

Because it reminds us of our animal origins, which we normally take great pains to conceal. We may love our dogs and cats, even to the point of treating them as substitute children, yet not for nothing is their Pal or Whiskas labelled 'Not suitable for human consumption'. Nor do we expect Fido to dine with a knife and fork. Frankly, his eating habits can be pretty disgusting, especially when he's wolfing down a rotting carcass in the park. Food and the way it is eaten most obviously dramatises the distinction between us and our animal friends.

When the infant Gargantua refuses to eat at the table, choosing to slurp his meals from a bowl on the floor with the family's hounds, it's a worrying sign of things to come. He, Pantagruel and Panurge are, to put it mildly, indelicate eaters. Their penchant for the bodily functions is positively depraved. Rabelais's books are, above all else, extended paeans to gorging and boozing – and the inevitable consequences. When Panatagruel farts, he makes the earth quake nine leagues around and 50,000 deformed little men are blasted out. His piss is copious enough to drown an entire city.

At one memorable point, our heroes literally go to war with battalions of heavily armed black-puddings, crusty pies and fat, sausage-like creatures called Chidlings, which they cut to pieces with the help of the ship's cooks and butchers. '... [A] fat and podgy woodland brain-meat Saveloy ran ahead in front of their battalion and tried to seize him by the throat. "By God," said Gymnaste, "you'll get in there only in slices." And so he pulled out his two-handled sword yclept *Kiss-me-arse* and sliced that Saveloy in twain. Good God, how fat was he! ... That Saveloy loyally savaged, the Chidlings rushed upon Gymnaste and threw him viciously to the ground just as Pantagruel and his men came running up to help at the double.'[54] Just when the battle is almost won, a gigantic flying pig, with crimson plumage, inflamed red eyes, green ears and a long, black tail like Lucullian marble, swoops down to scatter mustard over the battlefield, and the meats and Chidlings retreat in awe. As a take on the conflict between Carnival and Lent, this outdoes even Bruegel's.

Rabelais, of course, possesses an exceptional imagination, and not many authors can make food as vividly aggressive as he can. Not many have tried. Gogol's nose baked in a loaf of bread is curious rather than distasteful. Martin Amis comes close in *Lionel Asbo*, when a violent young thug is finally brought to heel in an up-market restaurant after a climactic struggle with a lobster. 'Next time, I'll have the haddock,' he muses, as his wounds are stitched up. Only the Portnoy family innocently sitting around the dinner table eating the liver that young Portnoy has earlier masturbated into can match the master for comic repugnance.

To experience the full comedy of gross consumption, you

have to be able to see it. A written description of the Young Ones getting down on the floor to scoop up spilt lentil stew can't begin to convey the hilarious horror of it, the filthy state of the carpet, for one thing, the fact that Vyvian has walked through the grey sludge in his bovver boots, or the enthusiasm with which the lads gobble it down. It's all just too awful for words.

Which leads us, inevitably, back to Monty Python. As the grotesquely obese Mr Creosote waddles into an up-market restaurant and lowers himself at his favourite table (in *Monty Python's The Meaning of Life*), we know we're in for something we'd rather not see. But it proves hard to look away. John Cleese is an obsequious waiter with an awful Frenchified accent, determined to cater to his most valued customer's every peccadillo, which includes vomiting copiously all over the floor. Unfazed, Cleese cheerfully calls for a bucket and a woman with a mop, while he explains the menu. She is vomited over, as are the menu and nearby diners. Soon the room is awash with thick yellow puddles of vomit, yet Cleese goes on helpfully recommending dishes to titillate Mr Creosote's tastebuds. Finally, it proves too much, even for the fat man himself. 'Fuck off, I'm full', he grumbles, as Cleese teases him with one last after-dinner mint. 'But Monsieur, ee's wafer-thin', he croons. When the mint is finally accepted, Cleese, knowing what's in store (because he's obviously been engineering it from the start, presumably out of sheer devilment), dives for cover behind the potted palms. The mint does the trick: Creosote explodes, showering the room with guts and half-digested food. In a final revolting touch, easy to miss amidst the mayhem, Cleese darts back to rescue the remains of the mint from Mr Creosote's exposed stomach and pops it triumphantly into his own mouth.

Perhaps this is meant as social satire, a comment on greed and the indulgent rich. But it is chiefly an outlandishly indulgent wallow in disgust for the sheer fun of it.

2 + 2 = 5

'Things fall apart; the centre cannot hold. Mere anarchy is loosed upon the world.' Although Yeats wasn't much taken with the prospect, for some it holds great promise. The comedy of entropy is a slap in the face of order and restraint. It demonstrates that even the most benign human activities, when taken to excess, are grotesque. It is necessary only to keep going when reason and good taste suggest you stop. There's a wicked pleasure to be had in witnessing the rigid, rule-bound systems that control our everyday lives thrown into disarray.

Only up to a point, however. Unless we are died-in-the-wool anarchists, we don't want our lives turned completely upside down, any more than the kids getting off on Sylvester and Tweety really want to do away with their parents. We just want to imagine what it would be like. We want to test the limits, to see how thin the carapace of civilisation is and what might lie beneath.

Two different responses are possible. At times of heightened anxiety, we are likely to picture entropy as something terrible. The dystopian visions of *Mad Max*, *Blade Runner* and *The Road* are a dire warning about the dangers of civilisation's collapse and the horrors of a world out of control. They play to our fears.

On the other hand, the optimistic sentiments of *I Love Lucy*,

Monty Python, the Marx Brothers and *Arrested Development* reveal the funny side of mayhem and misrule and the wonderful freedom they confer. They play to our mischievous side.

Neither should be confused with actuality, nor even wish-fulfilment. They are a kind of modelling. They ask the question 'What if?' when common wisdom says, 'Don't go there.' This is why the most popular examples, whether dystopian or optimistic, are the most extreme.

When push comes to shove, human nature, with all its imperfections, is still something we value over digital or mechanical regularity, even when it is irrational to do so. Although algorithms – and, for that matter, cogs and conveyor belts – deliver measurable results, we are reluctant to wholly place our trust in them. Which is why many people in a plane would baulk at the thought of an automated landing, insisting, at the very least, on human override.

It is our ability to entertain the idea of the impossible or irrational, and sometimes to choose it over the safe and predictable, that makes us fully human. In Dostoyevsky's novella *Notes from Underground*, the narrator observes that while 'two times two equals four' is an excellent thing, if everything is to be given its due, then 'two plus two equals five' is equally endearing. 'Two plus two equals five' is a completely irrational proposition, of course, yet by sometimes rejecting the materialist belief in a mechanical universe governed by verifiable physical laws, humankind boldly asserts its right to independence and exposes itself to possibilities.

Eight   THIS SILLY LIFE

Call them rebellious, unconventional, queer (in the old-fashioned sense), irresponsible or stark raving bonkers, there are those who choose to live the silly life, whether full- or part-time. They are few, because being at a slight angle to the universe is taxing and the rewards, sadly, are few.

As with most things, wealth (or at least the aura of wealth) will ease the way. Being English also helps. Mature, aristocratic Britishers of either sex, living alone with a retainer or two in a medieval castle or crumbling Tudor mansion, can happily take pot shots at visitors from upstairs windows, keep boa constrictors in their bathtubs or hang by their toes from oak trees without anybody so much as batting an eyelid. This is just the way the landed gentry is expected to behave. They are pretty useless anyway, so they might as well be entertaining.

Celebrities are also permitted to be habitually wayward with impunity. Michael Jackson's earning capacity was enhanced by his personal peculiarities, which were skilfully marketed. Hoarding bottles of Tabasco sauce, keeping a pet chimp and dangling babies from upstairs windows were all part of his mystique. Fame (like wealth, its close companion) marks a person out as different and special, allowing them to behave in ways that would otherwise be unacceptable. Besides, it's easy to treat life as one big joke when your position at the top of the social pile seems assured.

However, any welder, police constable or schoolmistress indulging such peccadillos will be discreetly whisked away, never to be seen again. Eccentricity among working people threatens to disrupt, rather than enhance, the smooth functioning of commerce.

On the whole, then, what we indulge as delightful eccentricity among aristocrats and the famous will usually be dismissed as madness in those of lower rank.

Getting up to no good

Tricksters, jokers and fools were the celebrities of the Renaissance. And, like the stars of today, they were typically people of modest talent and limitless ego. Sadly, they did not have the benefit of instant publicity. Their real fame was often posthumous, being dependent on someone publishing an account of their exploits long after their departure – nearly 200 years later in the case of the German, Till Eulenspiegel. He died in 1350, but the earliest-known complete edition of his pranks was published in 1515. Nevertheless, he did have quite a following during his lifetime, thanks in part to his extensive travels throughout Europe, performing tricks and jests wherever he went. Banksy-like, he left behind a little drawing of an owl and a mirror wherever he went, chalked on a wall or pavement (Eulenspiegel means 'owl mirror', suggesting 'wise reflection').

There is a fine line between a jest and a con, however. From a victim's point of view, a witty jape can look more like a vicious swindle. Till's tricks typically resulted in rich burghers, the nobility or the clergy getting their comeuppance, but all too often they targeted the poor and helpless and will strike most modern observers as cruel and vindictive. Renaissance humour was, to put it politely, a lot more robust than ours, often involving humiliation and physical injury. For example, having gathered an audience in a town square, Till talked a local priest into digging deep into a pot of gold, which, beneath a thin layer of coins, was full of fresh shit. That must have got a rousing reception. On another occasion, he mischievously promised a group of townsfolk a spectacular trick if they each tied one of their shoes to a length of cord. He then climbed up onto a tightrope, produced a pair of scissors and cut the shoes off, one by one, hurling them in all directions. He was probably the only one laughing as the poor sods hopped about searching for their footwear.

By way of compensation, Till also offered plenty of harmless jollity: song and dance, contortions, handstands and comic patter. Not knowing when the entertainment might take a nasty turn was presumably part of the attraction.

Nothing is known for certain about the life of another famous prankster of this period, the Englishman, John Scoggin. All we have is a biographical sketch in the introduction to his joke book, which was published in about 1570, nearly a century after his death. He is described as 'a man of honest birth and academical education who, by want of money, is reduced to great shifts, and who is not at all scrupulous as to the means of gaining his ends'. A con man, in other words. But a well-educated con man, indulged, and for a time employed, by the royal household.

Many of the pranks described in the book are simply baffling and will certainly fail to amuse anyone today. For example, he enters the queen's chamber and asks her if she wants a bit of horseplay. Yea, says she. So he pulls down his breeches, kicks with his heels, and calls, 'Wehee!' Then he asks his servant to do the same. 'Out, knave,' the queen shouts, and from then on she would have no horseplay in her chamber.

What on earth had she been expecting?

Others are more explicable and perhaps more in tune with modern sensibilities. Finding himself short of cash, Scoggin fills a box with white powder from a rotting fence and takes it to the parish church, telling the housewives gathered there that he has a potent flea-killer. They readily part with their money, take the powder home and sprinkle it among their bedclothes. Needless to say, it has no effect, so the next time they see Scoggin they angrily demand their money back.

> 'What sort of fools are you to buy something without asking how it should be used?' he sneers.
>
> 'Then how should we use it?' they ask.
>
> 'You must catch the flea, then, holding it carefully between your thumb and forefinger, force open its little mouth and pour the powder in.'
>
> 'Then,' say the women, throwing up their hands, 'we have not only lost our money, but we are mocked for our labours.'

Like many of Scoggin's victims, some of who suffered injuries, they appear to have given in without much of a fight.

Despite their unpleasantness, the earthy romps of Till Eulenspiegel, John Scoggin and others were valued for their supposed mental health benefits. Medical experts, worried that scholars and students, weighed down by their studies, were succumbing to melancholy, sensibly recommended a healthy dose of gaiety. It was not long before the taste for wild tales of dishonesty, insolence and knavery were translated from scholarly Latin into English for the middle classes, who were already well primed by the traditions of storytelling and popular song. And the books and pamphlets they responded to best were those that gathered the anecdotes under the name of a character famous for his wit and foolery, so as to suggest a continuous biographical narrative. Thus were sown the seeds of the modern novel. These men became, in the popular imagination, legendary figures of almost super-human abilities, like the movie heroes of today (although Eulenspiegel and Scoggin were more Joker than Batman).

Never mind that some of the tales cropped up again and again under different names, or that some dated back to ancient times, ordinary readers wanted to identify with a freewheeling character who could act out all their fantasies of a life without moral or physical constraint, in which priests, nobles and the gullible always came off second best.

Some travellers

In the early 1620s, the amateur poet John Taylor and his friend Roger Bird set out to row down the Thames for Queenborough in Kent (a distance of about 85 km). The boat was made entirely of brown paper, the oars of dried fish tied to lengths of cane. Taylor (who you may recall from chapter three as the inventor of the Barmoodan language) provides an account of the journey towards the end of his mock-epic poem, *The Praise of Hemp Seed*:

> *I therefore to conclude this much will note*
> *How I of Paper lately made a Boat,*

> *And how in forme of Paper I did row*
> *From London vnto Quinborough Ile show.*
> *I and a Vintner (Roger Bird by name)*
> *A man whom Fortune neuer yet could tame,*
> *Took ship vpon the vigill of Saint Iames*
> *And boldly ventur'd down the Riuer Thames.*

They endured a stormy night, their fragile craft disintegrating beneath them. 'And thus 'twixt doubt and feare, hope and despaire', he writes, 'I fell to worke, and *Roger Bird* to prayer'. While Roger prayed, the more practical Taylor inflated bulls' bladders he had thoughtfully brought along, and fixed them to the sides of the sodden craft. Thus, early the next morning, they washed up half dead at Queenborough where they were quickly revived by a cheering crowd and a civic reception.

The purpose of the journey was twofold: Taylor was keen to extol the virtues of hemp as a source of paper and cloth. In this, he was only partly successful, given that his boat turned to pulp. Mainly, though, it was a clever publicity stunt to promote sales of his poem. It was no accident that the mayor had a civic reception lined up for his arrival. It's all rather post-modern, in its way: writing a poem about a journey whose purpose is to promote the poem.

Taylor made eccentric travelling his specialty. Another of his epics is, THE PENNYLESS PILGRIMAGE, OR *The Money-lesse perambulation, of Iohn Taylor, Alias the Kings Majesties Water-Poet. HOW HE TRAVAILED ON FOOT From London to Edenborough in Scotland, not carrying any Money to or fro, neither Begging, Borrow-ing, or Asking Meate, drinke or Lodging. With his Description of his Entertainment in all places of his Iourney, and a true Report of the vnmatchable Hunting in the Brea of Marre and Badenoch in Scotland. With other Obseruations, some serious and worthy of Memory, and some merry and not hurtfull to be Remembred. Lastly that (which is Rare in a Trauailer) all is true.*

A title like that makes the poem seem redundant. 'The Penniless Pilgrimage', Taylor insists, was undertaken just for the hell of it: 'a trick of youth', as he puts it in his introduction. Yet, despite his claim that he did not beg or borrow, his extraordinary ability to profit from the generosity of strangers made the journey much less perilous than he would have us believe. Many of his sponsors refused to pay up, complaining that he had cheated. It was a decision they no doubt regretted when they found themselves mercilessly pilloried in a subsequent spray of Taylor doggerel.

Silliness is often a withering palimpsest: not satire, as such, but a jocular alternative aimed at reducing a serious and respected activity to absurdity. Taylor's travels can be seen in this light as a cheeky riposte to those of his contemporary, Thomas Coryat, with whom he appears to have enjoyed a vigorous love–hate relationship. Coryat (who also had a wicked sense of humour and made his living for a while as a sort of unofficial jester at the court of James I) was the greatest traveller of the age, covering much of Europe and parts of Asia, mostly on foot. For what it's worth, he is said to have introduced the table fork and the word 'umbrella' to England. Perhaps Taylor, knowing he could never compete with his rival, derived a certain satisfaction from making the very business of travel ridiculous, thus pulling the rug from under Coryat's well-worn feet. An ironic dedication to Coryat at the end of *The Praise of Hemp Seed* suggests as much.

Taylor is the forerunner of today's competitive, record-hunting travellers, striving to be the first legless man to climb Everest, or the first granny to jet ski up the Orinoco, or whatever it may be. The British comic book *Viz* had the mayor of Blackpool journeying to the South Pole by pedal boat to judge Captain Scott's snowman competition. To be noticed – for being noticed is usually the aim – the stunt must be physically punishing yet, apart from attracting attention, pointless (which I suppose puts the mayor of Blackpool's expedition out of contention). In other words, it must be fundamentally silly. It also needs to be something nobody has thought of before.

In 1895, for example, the Latvian–American journalist Annie Cohen Kopchovsky, or Annie Londonderry as she preferred, became the first woman to cycle around the world, spurred by a couple of misogynistic males who wagered that no woman was capable of such a feat. She was, it must be said, the most unlikely contender: not only a foreigner but a Jew (a distinct disadvantage in anti-Semitic Boston at the time), slightly built and a young mother of three. To top it off, she had never ridden a bicycle before and the one her sponsor provided was, by today's standards, almost unrideable.

But Annie had what all mad adventurers must have – guts, stubbornness, a genius for self-promotion and a cunning propensity to cheat when nobody was looking. One contemporary (a man, of course) sneered that she had gone around the world *with* a bicycle rather than on one, since ships and trains proved just as useful. Nevertheless, despite her exaggerations and dissembling, her achievement was a remarkable one and she won her $10,000 wager.

Yet fame built on such a flimsy pretext is bound to fade,

and Annie Londonderry's moment in the spotlight was disappointingly brief. Ventures of this kind are always subject to the law of diminishing returns, always vulnerable to being upstaged by the next, even more outrageous idea.

By now, it is hard to think of anything crazy enough to grab a headline. In 1998, Tony Hawks published his account of hitch-hiking around Ireland with (but not *on*) a refrigerator, which he called, appropriately enough, *Round Ireland with a Fridge*. It's hard to know whether this is an extreme example or a clever parody of the genre. Or is that a distinction without a difference?

Taylor, Londonderry and Hawks are seeking publicity and testing their endurance while at the same time enjoying a bit of a wheeze. For most thrillseekers of their kind, knowledge and understanding (except of themselves) are not high priorities.

They were for Charles Waterton, however. He was possessed of immense curiosity and kindness, combined with a ready wit and a frequently life-threatening sense of identification with all of God's creatures. Edith Sitwell, no slouch herself when it comes to eccentricity, praises Waterton's 'charm, goodness and fantastic gaiety'. 'He was an eccentric', she writes, 'only as all great gentlemen are eccentric, by which I mean that their gestures are not born to fit the conventions or the cowardice of the crowd ... and we may safely say that the world would be much better than it is if such eccentricity were more common'.[55] From 1812, Waterton undertook four hazardous expeditions through North and South America, where his pioneering studies of plants and animals would cement his modern reputation as a pioneer conservationist.

He liked to get up close and personal with his animal friends, at various times willingly sharing his bedroom with a boa constrictor, a crocodile (trussed, but even so), a toad and a vampire bat. He slept with his feet exposed in the hope the bat would suck his toes. In 1861, to the alarm of the keepers, he climbed into the orangutan cage at London Zoo to introduce himself to the inmates. Despite the alpha male's fearsome reputation, he seemed to appreciate the old man's good intentions and reciprocated with an affectionate hug.

Waterton's prose is beautifully evocative. Of his first encounter with a sloth in the jungle, he writes:

> He appears to us so forlorn and miserable, so ill put together is he, and so unfit to enjoy the blessings which have been so bountifully given to the rest of animated nature – for as it has formerly been remarked, he has no soles to his feet, and he is evidently ill at ease when he tries to move on the ground. It is then that he looks up in your face with a countenance that says, 'have pity on me, for I am in pain and sorrow'. Indeed, his looks and his gestures betray his uncomfortable situation, and, as a sigh every now and then escapes him, we may be entitled to conclude that he is actually in pain.[56]

At Walton Hall, his ancestral pile in Yorkshire, Waterton kept a sloth, which hung motionless for days on end from the back of a chair in his drawing room.

The extraordinary menagerie of wild creatures that freely wandered, flew and crawled around the corridors of Walton Hall constituted just one of many hazards that guests were likely to encounter. Even well into his eighties, Waterton was wont to insist that they join him on the highest branch of an oak tree to examine a bird's nest. Or they might find him teetering on the roof with a pair of homemade wings strapped to his arms (he was always talked down). As they hung their coats on the hall-stand, unsuspecting arrivals were sometimes alarmed by savage growling as a set of teeth sank painfully into their legs: it was the squire himself striving, through impersonation, to understand a dog's perspective (and playfully putting his guests on guard). When entertaining people who had not met him before, Waterton enjoyed appearing as a demented butler and chasing them around the dining room with a coal brush.

As if its living denizens were not enough to put people on edge, the house was dotted with stuffed creatures of monstrous appearance, which Waterton, skilled in taxidermy, had conjured up from various body parts. One had a face fashioned from a howler monkey's bottom. Although a bit worse for wear, it can still be seen in the old house, now open to the public. He delighted in naming these grotesques after well-known Protestants, he himself being a dedicated, if sceptical, Catholic.

Today, we are likely to separate Waterton's considerable achievements as an explorer and environmentalist from his personal eccentricities, full of admiration for the one and indulgently amused by the other. But, for most of his contemporaries, the consideration of animal welfare – the conviction that beetles, dogs, crocodiles and sloths were as deserving of compassion and understanding as any human – would have seemed just as preposterous, and quite possibly sacrilegious. The simple act of designing his stables so the horses could converse with one another would have marked Waterton out as decidedly odd. His silliness was prescient and only now, about a century-and-a-half later, is the rest of the world beginning to catch up with him.

Silliness can be fatal

John Taylor and Charles Waterton miraculously survived their many perilous escapades. It was as if an occult hand had guaranteed them protection. Others were less fortunate.

In his youth, Robert Louis Stevenson, author of *Treasure Island* and creator of Dr Jekyll and Mr Hyde, led a wild and dissolute life, mixing with some very dubious characters. They amused themselves in pubs and brothels with what they called jink, which involved 'doing the most absurd acts for the sake of their own absurdity and the consequent laughter'. Riotous 'blasphemy contests' were a favourite, which Stevenson, with his sound knowledge of the Christian faith, almost always won. It's just as well they were Scottish Presbyterians rather than, say, Muslims. One particularly close friend, a Frenchman named Eugene Chantrelle, took this anarchic spirit way too far. Although a man of wit, charm and literary ambition, he also liked to serve his guests toasted cheese flavoured with a lethal dose of opium. By this means he is thought to have dispatched about half-a-dozen innocent souls, including his unfortunate wife, before being caught and sentenced to death. Stevenson, who had had no idea of his friend's other life, later lamented that Chantrelle could have made a great success of almost anything he tried, had he not so often fallen back on 'the simpler plan' of killing people (although it could be said that he made a great success of that, at least for a while). Chantrelle is said to be the 'real' Dr Jekyll and Mr Hyde, although there are other contenders.

'I say that man is only so unfortunate because a thousand souls inhabit a single body.' Arthur Cravan's body – the tall, imposing frame of a heavyweight boxer – certainly contained many souls, the majority of them completely bogus. But I'm not sure why he thought this so unfortunate. I can only assume that he wasn't referring to himself but to anyone stupid enough not to be him. By failing to express their thousand souls and tying themselves to a single identity, people bring misfortune upon themselves. Consistency and predictability are the hallmarks of conformity. The silly life, in contrast, is multi-faceted. The skill to adopt a multiplicity of comic personae is just as essential to the success of the jester today as it was to Eulenspiegel and Scoggin. Cravan, a sort of modern-day Scoggin, fully embraced – or should that be indulged – his many souls.

Born in Switzerland in 1887, he adopted an English name, carried a British passport, yet spoke mainly French. He claimed to have lived in twenty countries (which seems highly unlikely), moving from one to another with fake documents under various assumed identities.

Despite an alarming number of scrapes and crises, all entirely of his own making, Cravan's various personas served him well; at least until, at the age of thirty-two, they got the better of him and he disappeared, never to be seen again. Cravan was many selves and no self. Or, as one contemporary put it, 'he never was the things he became'.

Although he had some talent as a writer, he produced very little, apart from some scurrilous art criticism and a small number of surrealistic poems. The main aim of his life, as he shamelessly admitted, was to infuriate people, get himself talked about and make his name. That was what earned him the admiration of Marcel Duchamp, Francis Picabia and André Breton, who declared him the father of Dada. Cravan set himself no goals and observed no limits, raising scandal, outrage and insult into an art form.

When entering the boxing ring, he insisted on being introduced as, 'The Mysterious Sir Arthur Cravan, the world's shortest-haired poet, grandson of the Chancellor to the Queen, of course, Oscar Wilde's nephew, likewise of course, and Alfred Lord Tennyson's great nephew, once again, of course: confidence man, sailor, snake charmer, hotel thief, lumberjack, chauffeur, and nephew to the Royal Commissioner into Welsh Sunday Closing'.[57] Some of this was true. He was certainly a confidence man, a thief and a sailor, for instance, and he was indeed Oscar Wilde's nephew (although the two never met). He was also, briefly, the French Amateur Light-Heavyweight Boxing Champion, which sounds impressive until you learn that, for one reason or another, all his opponents forfeited, so he earned the title without ever having to throw a punch.

Cravan was expelled from an English military academy for spanking a teacher, then got himself thrown out of Berlin on the official charge of being 'too noticeable'. Fortunately, the French proved more tolerant of noticeability and he became something of a local identity in his Parisian neighbourhood. When he loudly insulted people in bars and restaurants, even resorting to mild physical assault, most were admirably forbearing. They knew all about young Arthur and his crazy ways and were prepared to indulge him, which he must have taken as an intolerable affront to his hard-earned immaturity.

His public lectures were notorious. He would fire pistols at the ceiling, make insane pronouncements about art and life, balance first on one foot then the other, and shout insults at the audience, who appeared to relish the spectacle. The atmosphere soured on one occasion, though, when he threw his briefcase at them, narrowly avoiding injury.

If the sophisticated French mostly took such antics in their stride, the Americans were less forgiving. In 1916, Cravan fled to New York to avoid the draft, paying for his passage by staging a rigged boxing match with former World Champion, Jack Johnson. Unfortunately, the crowd twigged to the scam and Cravan just made it to the ship before they could catch up with him.

Waiting in New York was a whole new audience of eager innocents with a tendency to take themselves seriously, and thus gratifyingly susceptible to outrage. All the same, it was hardly unreasonable of a boxing match crowd to rise up jeering when, in the middle of a bout, Cravan subjected them to a lecture on Oscar Wilde. Invited to address the avant-garde Society of Independent Artists, he stripped naked (removing his clothes in public was something of a habit of his) and launched into a tirade of invective. A riot broke out and the police were called. It was one thing to shock the bourgeoisie, but shocking the Modernists was really an achievement.

It couldn't last, of course. And, when things got a bit overheated, Cravan did what he always did. He fled, this time to Mexico. A rather poignant letter has recently come to light in which he begs his lover, the poet Mina Loy, to join him there, threatening suicide if she doesn't. She relented, they married, and one day he climbed into a homemade rowboat and headed out toward the horizon and oblivion. Whatever might have become of his souls, which are probably still at large somewhere, his mortal remains were never found.

It was an oddly solitary and anti-climactic end for such a loud, rambunctious character, as if he had grown tired of playing the fool and was seeking some kind of reconciliation.

Silliness: A Serious History

There is something ineffably poignant about a man – especially this man – setting out alone in a frail vessel to surrender himself calmly to the overwhelming forces of nature. It is so much more ambiguous than, say, a bullet to the head or a leap from a ten-storey building. Doubts and speculations linger. Thus, Cravan stole a march on death, just as he had stolen a march on life.

These days, Cravan would probably be diagnosed as manic-depressive, and drugged, pacified and possibly incarcerated. His particular brand of madness is intolerable in an age of fearful conformity. Fortunately for him – or for his legacy, at least – the Dadaists didn't recognise the distinction between insanity and normalcy, or if they did, they plumbed for insanity.

Not all silly deaths are as affecting. Some are gloriously absurd. And there is a special award for those who accomplish what we might reasonably call the ultimate silliness.

But is 'silliness' the right word? Or are the Darwin Awards more about stupidity? Wendy Northcutt, the Awards' guiding spirit, certainly thinks so. 'In the spirit of Charles Darwin', she writes, 'the Darwin Awards commemorate individuals who protect our gene pool by making the ultimate sacrifice of their own lives. Darwin Award winners eliminate themselves in an extraordinarily idiotic manner, thereby improving our species' chances of long-term survival'. I'm sure Charles Darwin would be appalled on so many levels.

Would-be terrorist Khay Rahnajet was clearly not batting on a full wicket when he posted off a letter bomb without applying sufficient stamps. When it was returned to sender (did he really include his return address?), he was so pleased to be getting a parcel that he immediately tore it open, thus ending his career as a terrorist before it began and scoring him a well-deserved Darwin Award in 2000. Khay presents an unequivocal case of stupidity.

On the other hand, Lawnchair Larry, from Long Beach, California, was being harmlessly silly when he tied helium-filled weather balloons to a chair and took to the sky in 1982, floating serenely nearly 4000 metres above the ground. Unfortunately, from the Darwin Awards perspective, he survived, thus earning no more than an honourable mention, although it was perhaps some consolation that he was fined for violating commercial airspace.

It's not simply a matter of a stunt being silly if it succeeds but stupid when it goes horribly wrong. I think Ms Northcutt is missing a vital distinction. She should be more alert to the *intentions* of her awardees. Maybe she is right in maintaining that the stupid do us all a favour by occasionally taking themselves out of the gene pool (assuming, of course, that stupidity is entirely genetic, which is a pretty big assumption). Nevertheless, anyone sensitive to what's going on in the world can see that the gene pool could do with a lot more people prepared to treat so-called common sense with light-hearted disdain. In short, we need less stupidity but more silliness. There's a world of difference between Mr Rahnajet's sinister mission to blow people to pieces and Lawnchair Larry's loopy lark, and it does Larry a great disservice to lump him together with the stupid.

But it's not always clear cut. A 1995 winner, known only as Robert (is it any wonder that the vast majority of Darwin Award contenders are young males?) managed to be silly and stupid in equal measure. Riding a jet-ski over Niagara Falls was a wonderfully pointless and crazy thing to do, irrespective of the danger, and in line with all those thrillseekers who had earlier taken the plunge in barrels. Furthermore, Robert was prudent enough to equip his jet-ski with a rocket booster and to attach a parachute to his back. On the flip side, it was stupid of him not to notice that Niagara Falls is wet. The flooded rocket booster failed to ignite and his parachute wasn't waterproof. Robert's demise was spectacular.

Dada before Dada

The Dadaists are so often studied and written about that we are apt to think of them as more radical and original than they actually were. In fact, they were following a centuries-old tradition of collective, organised anarchy (if that's not a contradiction in terms). Although their precursors might not have been motivated by disgust, as the Dadaists were, they did at least express a healthy contempt for the norms, often at considerable personal risk.

For example, the eighteenth and early nineteenth centuries saw a flourishing of ugly clubs in Europe and America. Those who did not measure up to accepted standards of appearance, and who were tired of being mocked and attacked in the street, gathered together to rejoice in their ugliness, simultaneously mocking themselves and those who persecuted them. To gain membership to The Most Honourable and Facetious Society of Ugly Faces, founded in Liverpool in 1743, one had to be a bachelor and a man of honour with a facetious disposition who had, according to the club rules, 'something odd, remarkable, droll, or out of the way in his Phiz'. Ugly women, presumably, were on their own. Mr John Woods, for example, was admitted in 1751 for having a face 'altogether resembling a badger'. A carbuncle might earn you admission, so long as it was enormous, and prominent noses and long, pointy chins were a definite asset, 'especially if they should happen to meet together like a pair of nutcrackers'.[58]

In effect, it was a drinking club. Members met in pubs to sing and swap jokes, safe in the knowledge that they were not being harshly judged on their appearance. Nevertheless, in true eighteenth-century style, they kept meticulous records, which are mainly tongue-in-carbuncled-cheek.

Ugly clubs disappeared from America after the Civil War, when facial deformities no longer seemed funny, but I'm told they still exist in Italy as a cheeky riposte to the oppressive Italian cult of the beautiful.

There were also clubs and societies devoted to silliness of a more general nature. The best-known is The Nonsense Society, formed in Vienna in 1817 by a group of young artists, writers and musicians. It is remembered today chiefly because the composer Franz Schubert was one of its leading lights. Although we are apt to think of him as a tragic figure, dead at the age of 32 after a debilitating battle with syphilis, the young Franz was praised by a comrade as 'the soul and wit of the Society'.

All twenty-two members, male and female, were astonishingly prolific, organising absurdist debates, singing contests, costume parties and elaborately staged plays. They were very keen on cross-dressing and role-reversal and, in common with many such groups, they adopted childish pseudonyms, such as 'Big Snout', 'Sebastian Hairpowder' and (for one of the artists) 'Brushy Smearup'. This was partly for their own protection. Their gatherings, although they will strike us as perfectly harmless, were condemned as a threat to public order, making them vulnerable to police harassment. One can see why their antics might have unsettled the nervous regime. The implication, that nothing needed be taken seriously and that all rules and regulations were open to mockery, was an impertinence.

The Society's plays and pantomimes, for which Schubert wrote the music (the quirky little scherzo from the Piano Sonata no. 21 began life as a Nonsense Society contribution), were a wild mashup of surrealistic fantasy, bawdiness, wordplay and crude parody. As its newsletter, *The Archive of Human Nonsense*, reported about one chaotic performance: 'The actors competed honourably with each other, the choruses fell apart beyond all expectation and the piece disintegrated marvellously. What a wonder therefore that the performance ended with much laughter, art's beautiful reward.'[59]

They even anticipated Dada's famous alternative map of the world, in which countries are ranked in size according to how important they were deemed to be (Europe, needless to say, is tiny). *The Archive of Human Nonsense*, in a similar vein but a century earlier, published maps of Vienna dotted with punning street names, grotesquely phallic land features, and disembodied noses, ladders and other symbols which, if they had any meaning at all, were intelligible only to initiates.

There is strength in numbers. Banding together in a club or society is one way for those who are not rich, aristocratic or famous to be silly without the risk of being put in a straitjacket. Just the organisational skills needed to sustain a group, even one devoted to silliness, can give the impression of sanity. On the other hand, it also sets up a bigger target for despotic killjoys. The Nonsense Society was not the first or the last such group to be shut down by anxious rulers.

Dada after Dada

These days, of course, groups are just as likely to be virtual. No need for regular Thursday meetings in the local hall, no dress-up parties or stage performances. Just an indeterminate number of anonymous individuals sitting at home staring at a screen and occasionally pressing 'send' when the urge takes them. It's not the same, somehow. Even the original Nonsense Society has been recently revived as a website, although I'm sure Schubert and his cronies would think it a very pale imitation.

A Google search will throw up a plethora of oddly named organisations, although many turn out to be quite serious in intent. For example, although The Benevolent and Protective Order of Elks, in the US, sounds promising, it is in fact a genuine benevolent society that has counted senior politicians among its ranks. The Utter Pradesh Association of Dead People, despite its name, is anything but silly. It campaigns against a common fraud in that part of India, in which people are falsely reported dead so that relatives can claim their property. Given the seriousness of the cause, however, members adopt some admirably playful ploys, such as noisily and ostentatiously breaking the law, knowing that being arrested will force the authorities to admit they are alive.

It's hard to know how seriously the Pylon Appreciation Society (in the UK) takes itself. Members might well take exception to being called silly, even if appreciating pylons is something the rest of us might find a little odd. We are on much more secure ground with Gog Magog Molly, which originated at Cambridge University (most silly societies are university based, now as in the past: students have always done this sort of thing best). Members gather in bizarre costumes to dance in a style 'somewhere between nineties acid-house rave and Morris dancing', which could mean almost anything. The Twenty Minute Society, based at Newcastle University in the UK, carries on the noble tradition of organising comedy nights, performances, paintball sessions and other suitably anodyne entertainments, but with a delightfully pointless modern twist: members are notified of events by text only twenty minutes before they are due to begin: a sort of precursor of the flash mob.

The one I would most like to join is the Order of the Occult Hand. It comprises writers and journalists who have managed to sneak the phrase, 'It was as if an occult hand had ...' into whatever they are writing, without it being challenged by an eagle-eyed editor. Those who use the phrase repeatedly gain the most respect. It began in the USA in 1965 as a joke after a newspaper journalist had used it in all seriousness. 'It was as if an occult hand had reached down from above and moved the players like pawns upon some giant chessboard', he wrote, in a report about a man who had been mistakenly shot by his own family when he came home late. How the poor journalist must have come to regret his purple lapse. It wasn't long before occult hands were being facetiously evoked all over the world. In fact, so popular did they become that the Order has recently abandoned the phrase in favour of a new one, which they steadfastly refuse to reveal, thus adding another layer of pointlessness. Sadly, good editors are hard to find these days and those that there are do not work in journalism, which has rather taken the sport out of it.

In November 2016, a Melbourne man, Marcus Bowring, was issued a driver's licence. It was, in its way, a small victory for silliness. Most of us are embarrassed enough by our licence photos, which always look as if they'd caught us after an all-night vodka binge, but Mr Bowring compounded the problem by wearing a colander on his head for his. Surprisingly, VicRoads made no objection, saying – apparently with a straight bureaucratic face – that it respected all religious beliefs and the items of dress that hold special significance for them.

Religious beliefs? Well, Mr Bowring would insist on it. But the Church of the Flying Spaghetti Monster (aka Pastafarianism), signified by a colander on the head, is a religion only in the sense that it obviously isn't. Remarkably, it has been officially recognised as such by several countries, including New Zealand. What could they have been thinking? Don Quixote wore a basin on his head, thinking it was a helmet, but I'm not sure they would acknowledge the literary reference.

It all began by accident (as these things so often do) in 2005, when an American physics graduate, Bobby Henderson, wrote to the Kansas State Board of Education to protest against intelligent design being taught in schools alongside evolution. He made up a crazy religion by way of comparison, asking the board to demonstrate why it was any more absurd than intelligent design. While that might seem a specifically American concern, the basic principle – that the burden of proof lies with those who make unfalsifiable claims rather than with those who reject them – has wider application. The Church of the Flying Spaghetti Monster quickly became an internet phenomenon, and no one was more surprised than Mr Henderson. Not that he hasn't made the most of it since.

For the 'millions, if not thousands' of Pastafarians worldwide, a gigantic tangle of living spaghetti passing over an alcohol-spitting volcano gave rise to the earth as we know it. Since intelligent design posits an unidentified designer of some sort, the Flying Spaghetti Monster, Mr Henderson claimed, is surely as valid as any other.

Unlike other religions, the Pastafarians impose no restrictions. Instead of Ten Commandments, they have ten 'I'd rather you didn'ts', the only dogma being that there is no dogma (which makes you wonder why the Spaghetti Monster bothers with the 'I'd rather you didn'ts'). Wearing colanders and pirate costumes is a thing, but otherwise it's all pretty amorphous, as movements existing almost entirely in cyberspace necessarily are.

For no apparent reason, pirates ('those fun-loving buccaneers from history') play a central role. As the first Pastafarians, they are revered as divine beings. International Talk Like a Pirate Day, that dependable last resort of bored office workers everywhere, pays them due credit. Global warming is but one result of the lamentable decline in pirate numbers since the early 1800s. Somalia provides proof. It has the greatest number of pirates and the lowest carbon emissions in the world. QED.

The Church of the Flying Spaghetti Monster is a heady mix of satire, parody, carnivalesque subversion and sheer silliness. Limp pasta-related puns are a staple: 'r'amen', 'ramendan', 'pastover', and so on. If the stated aim is to show up the illogicality of what they call 'the crazy nonsense done in the name of religion' (the wording carefully avoids condemning religion as such), they are no less withering about science, as their theory of global warming and, of course, their creation myth demonstrate. Confusingly, Henderson says he looks forward to a world in which intelligent design, Pastafarianism and 'logical conjecture based on overwhelming observable evidence' are all given equal status.

In fact, the more you read about the Church of the Flying Spaghetti Monster, the more gloriously addled it gets. With thousands of otherwise unconnected people who rarely, if ever, meet or converse with one another and do not see themselves as bound by any regulations or restrictions, the result is bound to be an unholy muddle. Everyone wants a piece of the action, and who's to say that one contribution is any more valid than another?

Perhaps the Pastafarians are being sincere when insisting that their church is not a joke and has just as much legitimacy as all the rest, but much of what they do cheerfully undercuts the claim. Bobby Henderson created a monster in more ways than one. It has grown well beyond his original mission of exposing the absurdities of creationism and intelligent design to become a shining demonstration of just how complex, uncontrollable and unintelligible internet-enabled anarchy and absurdism can be. Somehow, through it all, the Pastafarians have managed to retain their collective sense of humour and high spirits, which is surely their most potent weapon and their most impressive achievement.

The devilish role of silliness

The Charles Watertons, Arthur Cravans and Lawnchair Larries of this world have a peculiar relationship to the rest of us, dancing a never-ending tango with the majority view. Despite their great show of non-conformity, such individuals depend on a measure of social response and some indulgence. Holding the norms up to ridicule works best when those norms are accommodating enough to bend a little in the breeze. The aim, after all, is not to bring the whole edifice down – that's the job of the revolutionary – but simply to luxuriate in its absurdity. Silly people are slightly apart from the world, but still of it.

Nineteenth-century rural Yorkshire, with its rigid social hierarchies and conservatism, proved a hospitable environment for Charles Waterton and his amiable dottiness. His money and position, and his great learning, protected him, serving both as a springboard and a safety net for his antics. Most people probably regarded him as a harmless old duffer (although he was much more than that). And, while he enjoyed taking the mickey out of the Anglicans, it was surely Protestant tolerance and accommodation of difference that made his existence relatively trouble-free. He was lucky.

The more hidebound and traditionalist the society, the more effective silliness will be, the more it will stand out and be noticed. This is why silliness today, despite its flourishing, has lost a lot of its sting – really, who cares any more? Anything goes. On the other hand, conservative societies are, by their very nature, fearful and intolerant of disruption, making even the most innocuous pranks risky. As we saw in the tragic case of Daniil Kharms in chapter four, to take an extreme example, silliness and authoritarianism do not make a good mix.

Being noticed is the aim of the game, and the more outrageous the behaviour (in the context of what's going on around it), the more attention the perpetrator can expect. In the early 1800s, when the poet Gérard de Nerval took his pet lobster for a walk in the gardens of the Palais Royale (where else?), it wasn't because the lobster needed the exercise. His protestations of love for the creature, who, he pompously declared, 'knew the secrets of the sea', could not disguise the fact that de Nerval was a show-off who craved the admiration and affection of his peers and the scandalised disapproval of those he didn't care about – provided, of course, that everyone recognised it as a game and none felt threatened (the lobster, presumably, wasn't consulted).

While we will enjoy hearing about John Taylor risking life and limb in a paper boat, or Charles Waterton sharing his bedroom with a crocodile, or even the Pastafarians holding themselves up to public ridicule, we don't necessarily want to take those risks ourselves. These people are being silly on our behalf, and, if we are properly attentive, we will be grateful for their sacrifices. As the playwright Michael Frayn once pointed out, farce is defined by panic and, while we are all afraid of losing control in life, it's funny when it's happening to someone else. Especially, I would add, when it is bracketed off as a performance.

However, a playful up-yours to social standards and assumptions is more than just the empty swagger of the self-publicist. Habitual pranksters are not just making spectacles of themselves. Whether consciously or otherwise, they are going back to root causes and first principles, not to picture a better future but simply to release us, for a while, from habit. These happy souls are disruptive and sometimes, as with Arthur Cravan, offensive, but most often they are funny because they make us laugh at ourselves. By connecting with childhood, madness and the primitive, they uncover something of the essence of human experience.

Silliness, therefore, however much it might insist on being

pointless, has its devilish role to play. Since ancient times, all cultures and societies have indulged in it (or at least tolerated it). Occasionally – as in the sixteenth and eighteenth centuries – it has flourished. By poking fun at rules and restrictions, dismissing the powerful with an airy wave and turning logic on its head, silliness summons laughter and points the way to freedom.

How extraordinary that something apparently so useless can turn out to be so important. And rarely has it been so important, indeed so necessary, as it is today.

NOTES

1 Quoted by James Kaplan, in 'The Laughing Game', *New Yorker*, 7 February 2000
2 Coe, Jonathan, *Number 11*, London, Viking, 2015
3 Rabelais, *Gargantua and Pantagruel*, London, Penguin Classics, 2006, p. XXXIV
4 Hansen (ed.), *The Book of Greek and Roman Folktales, Legends and Myths*, Princeton University Press, 2017
5 Aristophanes, *The Birds and Other Plays*, London, Penguin Classics, 2003, pp. 206–207
6 Aristophanes, *Frogs and Other Plays*, London, Penguin Classics, 2007, p. 186
7 Otto, Beatrice, *Fools are Everywhere*, Chicago, University of Chicago Press, 2007, pp. 234 & 236
8 Rabelais, *Gargantua and Pantagruel*, London, Penguin Classics, 2006, p. 86
9 *ibid.*, p. 24
10 Sterne, Laurence, *The Life and Opinions of Tristram Shandy, Gentleman*, London, Penguin English Library, 1967, p. 87
11 Westbury et al., 'Telling the world's least funny jokes: on the quantification of humor as entropy', in *Journal of Memory and Language*, no 86, 2016, pp. 141–156
12 *ibid.*, p. 141
13 Lewis, C.S., *The Pilgrim's Regress*, Michigan and Cambridge, William B. Eerdmans, 2014, p. 47
14 James, Clive, *Unreliable Memoirs*, London, Picador Classics, 2015, p. 6
15 Quoted in Schmalenbach, Werner, *Kurt Schwitters*, London, Thames and Hudson, 1970, p. 212

16 *ibid.*, p. 232
17 Opie, I. & P., *The Oxford Dictionary of Nursery Rhymes*, Oxford University Press, 1988, p. 261
18 Aristophanes, 'Frogs', in *Frogs and Other Plays*, London, Penguin Classics, 2007, p. 141
19 Rabelais, *Gargantua and Pantagruel*, *op. cit.*, pp. 34 & 36
20 *ibid.*, p. 509
21 online at unterseher.com
22 Tindall, W., *A Reader's Guide to Finnegans Wake*, London, Thames and Hudson, 1969, p. 32
23 Swift, Jonathan, 'A Modest Defence of Punning', in *A Modest Proposal and Other Writings*, Penguin Classics, 2009, p. 95
24 Tovey, Beth, 'Why Lear's "nonsense" language is more than just fun', OxfordWords blog, blog.oxforddictionaries.com
25 Milligan, Spike, 'On the Ning Nang Nong', in *Silly Verse for Kids*, London, Penguin, 1973
26 O'Brien, Flann, *The Third Policeman*, London, Harper Perennial, 2007, pp. 62–63
27 Cook, Peter, *Tragically, I was an only Twin*, Arrow Books, 2003, pp. 309–310
28 Micallef, Shaun, *Mad as Hell*, series 7, episode 5, ABC Television
29 Snicket, Lemony, *A Series of Unfortunate Events: The Grim Grotto*, London, Egmont, 2016, pp. 62 & 63
30 'Manifesto of the Futurist Painters', 1910, in Apollonio, Umbro (ed.), *Futurist Manifestos*, London, Thames and Hudson, 1973
31 Kharms, Daniil, *Today I Wrote Nothing*, New York, Ardis, 2009, p. 16
32 Quoted in Blasdel, Alex, 'The Anthropocene Age of Reckoning', in *Guardian Weekly*, 14 July 2017, p. 31
33 *Times Literary Supplement*, 25 March 2016, p. 18
34 Sterne, Laurence, *The Life and Opinions of Tristram Shandy*, London, Penguin Classics, 1980, p. 286
35 Gorey, Edward, *The Listing Attic and the Unstrung Harp*, London, Abelard, 1974, n.p.
36 Translated by Robert Dessaix
37 O'Brien, Flann, *At Swim-Two-Birds*, London, Penguin Modern Classics, pp. 100–101
38 *The George Burns and Gracie Allen Show*, online at YouTube

Notes

39 online at www.ibras.dk/montypython/episode08.htm
40 Rabelais, *op. cit.*, pp. 39–44
41 *ibid.*, pp. 163–164
42 *ibid.*, p. 241
43 *ibid.*, p. 269
44 *ibid.*, p. 406
45 Lemony Snicket, *The Reptile Room*, London, Egmont Books, 2012, p. 155
46 Lemony Snicket, *The Bad Beginning*, London, Egmont Books, 2012, p. 11
47 Joyce, James, *Finnegans Wake*, London, Faber and Faber, 1975, pp. 71–72
48 *ibid.*, p. 104
49 Beckett, Samuel, *Watt*, London, Faber and Faber, 2009, p. 93
50 Quoted in Hansen, A., 'Entropy and Transformation', in Boskin, Joseph (ed.), *The Humor Prism in 20th Century America*, Detroit, Wayne State University Press, 1997, p. 59
51 Marx Brothers, *Animal Crackers*, Paramount Pictures, 1930, Universal Pictures and Umbrella Entertainment DVD
52 Aristophanes, *Frogs and Other Plays*, Penguin Classics, 2007, p. 44
53 Cook, Peter, *Tragically I was an Only Twin*, Arrow Books, 2003, p. 275
54 Rabelais, *Gargantua and Pantagruel: the Fourth Book of Pantagruel*, London, Penguin, 2006, p. 785
55 Sitwell, Edith, *English Eccentrics*, London, Penguin, 1980 edition, p. 246
56 Quoted in Sitwell, *ibid.*, pp. 233–234
57 Quoted in Jones, Dafydd (ed.), *Dada Culture: Critical Texts on the Avant Garde*, 2006, Rodopi, p. 201
58 'Ye ugly face clubb, Leverpoole, 1743–1753: a verbatim reprint from the original ms. in the collection of the late Joseph Mayer, esq., of Bebington, Cheshire / (Liverpool: Edward Howell, 1912), by Edward Howell', *onlinebooks.library.upenn.edu*
59 Quoted in Stebin, Rita, *Schubert: the Nonsense Society Revisited*, Assets Press, Princeton University, 2014, p. 12

Index

Specific works are listed under the names of their creators or the individual generally associated with them. So, for *Alice in Wonderland* see 'Lewis Carroll'. The exceptions are when the creators are unknown or not widely recognised: for example, *Arrested Development* or *I Tawt I Taw a Puddy Tat*.

A
Abbott and Costello 159–161
Adams, Phillip 99
Allen, Gracie 134–135
Allen, Woody 135–136
Amis, Martin 193
animal noises 61–66
Aquinas, Thomas 15
Arbuckle, Fatty 170
Archive of Human Nonsense 216
Aristophanes 22–25, 26, 64–65, 73–74, 131, 186
Aristotle 11
Arrested Development 110, 183–185, 196
Auster, Paul 158

B
Ball, Hugo 58–59
Ball, Lucille 134, 165, 166, 180–182, 195
Bean, Mr. 13, 165, 166
Beard, Mary 27
Beckett, Samuel 40, 44, 88, 98, 102–105, 109, 139, 158–159, 161
Black Books 110
Bloom, Harold 114, 117
Borge, Victor 4, 123
Britten, Benjamin 145

Brooks, Mel 4, 135
Bruce, Lenny 14
Bruegel, Pieter 33–34
brussels sprout, world's biggest 140
Bugs Bunny 32, 139, 176
Burns, George 134–135

C
Cage, John, 148
Calloway, Cab 60–61
Carnival 33–35, 100
Carroll, Lewis 44–46, 51–52, 53–54, 78, 79–80, 81, 83, 88, 99–100, 106
cartoons 176–178, 179
Cervantes, Miguel (*Don Quixote*) 39, 114–17, 119, 120, 126
Chantrelle, Eugene 208
Chaplin, Charlie 49, 165–168, 170, 172, 173, 179–180, 181
Cheech and Chong 161–162
Chekhov, Anton 165
Chesterton, G.K. 45, 46
children 6, 10, 15, 18, 19, 45–46, 50–51, 52, 57–58, 61–64, 81, 84, 85, 98, 112, 120–121, 144–148, 162–163, 176–177, 191
Church of the Flying Spaghetti Monster, see 'Pastafarianism'

Index

Cicero 73–74
Cleese, John 5, 17, 187, 194
Coe, Jonathan 7
Comenius, John 61–62
commedia dell'arte 36–37, 51
Cook, Peter 7, 50, 89–90, 94–95, 96, 107, 187
copreae 27, 51
Coryat, Thomas 65, 203
Courtneidge, Cicely 155
Cravan, Arthur 208–212, 221, 223
Crum, Paul 17

D
Dada 46–48, 58–60, 209, 212, 214, 216
Dahl, Roald 53, 78, 79, 83–85
Darwin Awards, 212–214
de Nerval, Gérard 222–223
Dostoyevsky, Fyodor 196
dreams 94
Dumont, Margaret 174–175, 184
Dylan, Bob 4, 5, 13–14

E
Ehrenreich, Barbara 35
Eliot, T.S. 80
Elton, Ben 108
entropy 164–196
Eulenspiegel, Till 198–199, 200–201, 209

F
Farrelly Brothers (*There's Something About Mary*) 188–189
Fast Show, The 146
Fermor, Patrick Leigh 65
Fey, Tina (*30 Rock*) 110, 185
fools, see jesters
Foote, Samuel 87–88

Frayn, Michael 223
Freud, Sigmund 14, 17, 18, 110
Fry, Stephen 154
Futurists 102

G
genre 4, 13
Gervais, Ricky (*Extras*) 14–15
gibberish 56–61
Glass, Philip 150
Gog Magog Molly 217–218
Gogol, Nikolai 44, 93, 105, 126–129, 193
Goodall, Howard 123
Goons 5, 81–82
Gorey, Edward 124
gross-out comedy 188–191
Groundhog Day 151–152
Gunston, Norman 20–21

H
Hausmann, Raoul 59
Hawks, Tony 205
Haydn, Joseph 5, 121–122, 123
Hellzapoppin 132–133, 184
Henderson, Bobby 219–220, 221
Hill, Benny 76, 166
hip-hop 61
Honest Whore, The 91

I
Iannucci, Armando 7–8
Ife, B.W. 116
Incongruity Theory 13–14, 17, 55, 110
International Talk Like a Pirate Day 220
I Tawt I Taw a Puddy Tat 177–178
internet 50, 110–111, 154, 185, 220–221
Ionesco, Eugène 44

J

Jackson, Michael 197
James, Clive 58
James, William 55
Jarmusch, Jim 160
Jarry, Alfred (*Ubu Roi*) 100–102, 107
jayus 184
jesters 27, 29–31, 32, 51, 74, 198–201
jink 208
Johnson, Doctor 74
Jokes 1–2, 13, 18, 26–27, 182–185
Joyce, James 40, 44, 55–56, 70–72, 78, 79, 85, 88, 109, 131, 155–158, 162

K

Kant, Immanuel 13, 17
Keaton, Buster 49, 167, 168–169, 170, 171, 173, 181
Keystone Cops 49, 102
Kharms, Daniil 105–107, 109, 222
Kierkegaard, Søren 13, 17
Krazy Kat 102, 132

L

Laurel and Hardy 164–165, 168, 169, 171–172, 191
Lawnchair Larry 213, 221
Lear, Edward 5, 25, 45–46, 51–52, 79, 80, 81, 82, 83, 88, 124–126, 146
Lester, Richard (*How I Won the War*) 189–190
Lewis, C.S. 57–58
Lewis, Jerry 3
limericks 4–5
Little Britain 150–151, 159
Lloyd, Harold 165, 167, 168, 170–171
Londonderry, Annie 204–205
Looney Tunes 94
Lumière Brothers 48

M

marginalia (in medieval manuscripts) 28
Marx Brothers 132, 165, 172–175, 176, 182, 183, 184, 196
Marx, Groucho 73, 132, 173, 174
Mayall, Rik 108
Mayer, Lise 108
Méliès, Georges (*A Trip to the Moon*) 48–49, 50
Micallef, Shaun, 95–97
Milligan, Spike, 17, 20, 81–83, 89
mise-en-abyme 112–137
Monty Python 10, 11, 92, 138–140, 190–191, 196
Moore, Dudley 95, 123–124
Morton, Ian 111
Mozart, W.A. 5, 122
Murdoch, Rupert 77

N

Nietzsche, Friedrich 43
Nonsense Society 215–217
non sequiturs 87–111
Northcutt, Wendy 212, 213
nursery rhymes 92–93, 119–121, 144–147

O

O'Brien, Flann (*At Swim-Two-Birds*) 25, 93, 129–13, 187
Oh! What a Lovely War 46
Order of the Occult Hand 218
Otto, Beatrice 30–31

P

pantomime 37–38, 131
Pastafarianism 219–221, 223
Plautus 25–26, 36, 73, 131–132
play 15–16
Plutarch 23, 57

Index

Pollack, John 73
portmanteau words 78–79
Prix de la Page 112 19
puns 72–78
Pylon Appreciation Society 217

R

Rabelais, François (*Gargantua and Pantagruel*) 21, 25, 38–40, 56–57, 66–67, 68, 79, 85, 93, 140–144, 149–150, 158, 192–193
Rahnajet, Khay 212–213
Raymond, Louis 4
recursion 156
redundancy 138–161
Release Theory 14–15, 110
repetition 138–161
Robert 213–214
Roland the Farter 29
Russell, Anna 123

S

Sacks, Oliver 144
Salinger, J.D. 128
Satie, Eric 148–149
satire 7–9, 20, 183
Scheerbart, Paul 58
Schopenhauer, Arthur 13, 17, 55
Schubert, Franz 215–216
Schwitters, Kurt 47, 59–60
Scoggin, John 29–30, 40, 199–201, 209
Screech, M.A. 21, 66
Screaming Lord Sutch 8
Shakespeare, William 68–70, 79
Sheridan, Thomas 75
silent movies 48–50, 165–171
Simpsons, The 79, 150, 163
Sinatra, Frank 148
Sitwell, Edith 205
skaz 126–131

slapstick 37, 55, 107, 166–168, 182, 188, 189
Snicket, Lemony 97–98, 147, 149, 163
Sterne, Laurence (*Tristram Shandy*) 25, 41–43, 107, 117–119, 127
Stevenson, Robert Louis 208
Stoppard, Tom 136
stupidity 9–11, 139–140, 212–214
Superiority Theory 11–13
Swift, Jonathan 70, 74–75, 85–86
Sydney Front, The 192
Symons, Arthur 101

T

Taylor, John 65–66, 68, 201–204, 205, 208, 223
Thick of It, The 8
Three Stooges 191
Thurber, James 17–18
Tindall, William 71, 156
tongue-twisters 152–155
Trickster 31–32, 51, 158
Twenty Minute Society 218
Two Ronnies, The 75–76, 155

U

ugly clubs, 214–215

V

Vaudeville 102, 160, 188
Velázquez, Diego 112, 113

W

Waterton, Charles 205–207, 208, 221–222, 223

Y

Young Ones, The 107–109, 188, 191, 194
YouTube 51, 59, 69, 160, 178

Wakefield Press is an independent publishing and
distribution company based in Adelaide, South Australia.
We love good stories and publish beautiful books.
To see our full range of books, please visit our website at
www.wakefieldpress.com.au
where all titles are available for purchase.
To keep up with our latest releases, news and events,
subscribe to our monthly newsletter.

Find us!

Facebook: www.facebook.com/wakefield.press
Twitter: www.twitter.com/wakefieldpress
Instagram: www.instagram.com/wakefieldpress

www.ingramcontent.com/pod-product-compliance
Lightning Source LLC
Chambersburg PA
CBHW030106170426
43198CB00009B/507